# The Green Guide to Specification

# The Green Guide to Specification

# an Environmental Profiling System for Building Materials and Components

# Third Edition

Jane Anderson
Building Research Establishment Ltd

David E. Shiers
Oxford Brookes University

*with*

Mike Sinclair
Consignia

**Blackwell
Science**

© 2002 by
Consignia, Oxford Brookes University and The Building Research
Establishment

Blackwell Science Ltd
Editorial Offices:
Osney Mead, Oxford OX2 0EL
25 John Street, London WC1N 2BS
23 Ainslie Place, Edinburgh EH3 6AJ
350 Main Street, Malden
  MA 02148 5018, USA
54 University Street, Carlton
  Victoria 3053, Australia
10, rue Casimir Delavigne
  75006 Paris, France

Other Editorial Offices:

Blackwell Wissenschafts-Verlag GmbH
Kurfürstendamm 57
10707 Berlin, Germany

Blackwell Science KK
MG Kodenmacho Building
7-10 Kodenmacho Nihombashi
Chuo-ku, Tokyo 104, Japan

Iowa State University Press
A Blackwell Science Company
2121 S. State Avenue
Ames, Iowa 50014-8300, USA

First published 2002

Set in 9/14 Trebuchet
by DP Photosetting, Aylesbury, Bucks
Printed and bound in Great Britain by
MPG Books Ltd, Bodmin, Cornwall

The Blackwell Science logo is a trade mark of Blackwell Science
Ltd, registered at the United Kingdom Trade Marks Registry

Produced on Elemental chlorine-free paper.

DISTRIBUTORS

  Marston Book Services Ltd
  PO Box 269
  Abingdon
  Oxon OX14 4YN
  (*Orders*:  Tel: 01235 465500
              Fax: 01235 465555)

USA
  Blackwell Science, Inc.
  Commerce Place
  350 Main Street
  Malden, MA 02148 5018
  (*Orders*:  Tel: 800 759 6102
                   781 388 8250
              Fax: 781 388 8255)

Canada
  Login Brothers Book Company
  324 Saulteaux Crescent
  Winnipeg, Manitoba R3J 3T2
  (*Orders*:  Tel: 204 837-3987
              Fax: 204 837-3116)

Australia
  Blackwell Science Pty Ltd
  54 University Street
  Carlton, Victoria 3053
  (*Orders*:  Tel: 03 9347 0300
              Fax: 03 9347 5001)

A catalogue record for this title is available
from the British Library

ISBN 0-632-05961-3

Library of Congress
Cataloging-in-Publication Data
is available

For further information on
Blackwell Science, visit our website:
www.blackwell-science.com

# Contents

# Foreword

The original purpose of this handbook was to raise the awareness of construction professionals employed within the industry to the environmental issues involved in the specification of building materials and so promote 'best practice' in the procurement and management of The Post Office's (now Consignia's) extensive property portfolio.

Few professionals are in a position to research the production processes and environmental impacts of each of the many materials used in the building process, and prior to the first edition of this book, there was no single, comprehensive source of information on the subject. For this reason, in 1992, following the launch of Consignia's Environmental Impact Policy, Property Holdings embarked on research into the development of an environmental profiling system for materials and components used in building, and this, the third edition of *The Green Guide to Specification*, is the culmination of this initiative.

The production of this handbook would not have been possible without the involvement of Oxford Brookes University, and thanks are due in particular to David Shiers for the design and development of the Profiling System and for leading the original project. As part of the original team that put together the first two editions, special thanks are due to Nigel Howard, whose expertise and specialist knowledge afforded access to and interpretation of the extensive databases required for such a project.

The team is also indebted to Jane Anderson of BRE for her ability to smoothly take over where Nigel left off, synthesising complex tasks into clear and easy-to-follow steps. These inputs enabled our original vision to become a reality.

Our environment is significantly affected by the production and use of materials. The goal of this book is to take something complex and make it simple to understand. I hope this book has achieved this goal and makes a positive contribution towards ensuring that sound environmental choices are made.

Mike Sinclair
Head of Building Programmes
Consignia

# Acknowledgements

We wish to acknowledge the contributions made by the following individuals and organisations:

Dr Brenda Boardman and the Environmental Change Unit,
University of Oxford
Deborah Brownhill, BRE
Centre for Whole Life Performance, BRE
Suzy Edwards, BRE
Steve Garvin, BRE
Dr Karen Kearley
Miles Keeping, Oxford Brookes University
Professor Anthony Lavers, Oxford Brookes University
Kate Mills, BRE

Dr Geoff Milne
Chris Newman, BRE
The Trevor Patrick Partnership
Gerry Saunders, BRE
Dr Sarah Stevens
Alan Yates, BRE
Tony Yates, BRE

Special thanks are due to Nigel Howard for his contributions
to this project.

# The Authors

## Jane Anderson BA, MSc

Jane Anderson has been a consultant with the Centre for Sustainable Construction at BRE since 1998. Her expertise lies in the development and application of Life Cycle Assessment methodology to construction materials, components and buildings. She has an architecture degree and gained a distinction in her Masters in Architecture from the University of East London.

Together with Nigel Howard and Suzy Edwards, she developed the BRE Environmental Profiles Methodology, published in 1999, and was responsible for the development of the IT systems used to calculate and provide BRE Environmental Profiles. In 2000, she was a co-author of *The Green Guide to Housing Specification*, a version of the *Green Guide* specifically targeted at elements and specifications used in housing.

She continues to manage the provision of BRE Environmental Profiles for product manufacturers and trade associations, and to work on the development of new tools to provide architects and specifiers with simple tools to reduce the embodied impacts of their buildings.

## David Shiers BA, BArch Hons (L'pool), CertHE, RIBA

David Shiers is a qualified architect and Principal Lecturer in Development, Design and Construction at the Centre for Real Estate Management, Oxford Brookes University. He is a graduate of the Liverpool University School of Architecture and spent 12 years in private practice working on a wide range of commercial and residential projects as a designer and project manager. He has written extensively on many aspects of property-related environmental issues, including the property investment implications of sustainable development, occupier demand for 'green' buildings and the environmental impact of building materials.

David has been involved with the *Green Guide* project since 1993 and designed the original Environmental Profiling System still used as the methodological basis of the current edition. He was the co-author of the first and second editions of *The Green Guide to Specification*, with Nigel Howard of BRE and Mike Sinclair of Consignia Property Holdings, the second edition being launched by the Minister for the Construction Industry, Nick Raynsford MP, in September 1998, as part of BREEAM 98 for Offices. He is also a member of the international working commission on sustainable construction, CIB W-100: The Environmental Assessment of Buildings.

## Mike Sinclair FRSA, FBIFM, FRICS, MBEng

Mike Sinclair is Head of Building Programmes with Consignia. He is currently responsible for the delivery of Consignia's capital and maintenance building programmes throughout the UK. Mike has held many positions within Consignia (formerly The Post Office) including Head of Construction and Facilities, during which time he conceived the idea for the first edition of *The Green Guide to Specification*. Since qualifying as a Building Surveyor in 1976 Mike has held senior posts in Buckinghamshire County Council, Travis & Arnold Plc and was an Associate with Edmund Kirby & Sons prior to joining Consignia.

He is a Fellow of the Royal Institution of Chartered Surveyors, Fellow of the British Institute of Facilities Management, Member of the Association of Building Engineers and a Fellow of the Royal Society of Arts.

He has published articles in *Chartered Surveyor Monthly*, *Building* magazine and various building publications marketed by Excel Publishing, on the *Green Guide*, Disability Discrimination Act and other construction-related subjects affecting both Consignia and the construction industry in general.

# Part I
# Introduction

## A global issue

As awareness of the potential environmental impacts from the production, use and disposal of building materials has grown, many designers, property owners and other construction professionals have sought to take a more environmentally responsible approach to the selection and specification of materials.

Around 30% of UK industrial energy is consumed annually in the manufacture and transport of building materials which equates to approximately 10% of all UK energy consumption (CIRIA, 1994). There is mounting evidence to suggest that the concentrations of $CO_2$ (Carbon Dioxide) and other 'greenhouse' gases (such as methane) in the atmosphere are increasing. This, it is argued, is leading to global warming and climate change. As the main source of these greenhouse gases is the burning of fossil fuels for energy, a reduction in the energy levels required in the manufacture of building materials represents an opportunity for materials producers to minimise the environmental impact of their products. Designers and specifiers can assist in this process through more environmentally responsible choices.

The UK Government is a signatory to the 1997 Kyoto Conference agreement, where most of the world's developed countries agreed to cut the emissions of greenhouse gases by an average of 5.2% on 1990 levels between 2008 and 2012. The UK's stated target is to reduce $CO_2$ emissions to a level of 20% less than the 1990 figures by 2010. Whilst the Government has to date pursued these objectives through voluntary schemes, it seems increasingly likely that compliance will be sought through legislation and tax measures. The introduction of the Climate Change Levy (CCL) on business energy use is one example of this approach.

In terms of the manufacture of building products, the release of chemicals into the atmosphere from production processes has been linked to damage to the ozone layer and to other effects harmful to the environment and human health. VOC (volatile organic compound) emissions may be irritant or toxic. $NO_x$ (nitrogen dioxide and nitrogen oxide), released in combustion processes, is both a contributor to acid rain and reacts with VOCs in sunlight to produce photochemical smog. This smog is implicated in increased incidence of asthma and respiratory illness. $SO_2$ (sulphur dioxide), also released from the combustion of oil and coal products, is the main contributor to acid rain. Electricity generation in the UK is a major user of fossil fuels and thus electricity use also results in high levels of these polluting gas emissions.

A reduction in construction and demolition waste has also been identified as a priority by the UK Government. At present, over 90% of non-energy minerals extracted in Great Britain are destined for use as construction materials, and each year, around 70 million tonnes of construction and demolition waste is generated, of which around 13 million tonnes is materials delivered to site and thrown away unused.

Many in the property industry are aware of the need to further reduce exposure to 'environmental risk'. Whilst the most common construction- and development-related risks have been associated with polluting activities or the failure of specialists to deal with specific environmental hazards, the future scope of environmental liability may have far-reaching implications for the construction industry. The impact of the construction process in terms of energy use or levels of emissions on global conditions could be identified as a major 'indirect' environmental hazard. As such, it is possible that these issues will become potential legal liability flashpoints and that designers, specifiers and materials manufacturers will be obliged to take this into account in the design and construction process.

Property investors and funding institutions, under pressure from shareholders and insurers, are also seeking a 'greener' and more 'socially responsible' approach to the design and procurement of buildings. A more carefully considered, environmentally aware approach to the specification of materials is important in being able to demonstrate that projects are well managed, responsible and are protecting shareholders' interests through minimising the risks associated with environmental impact.

## The purpose of this book

Prior to the publication of the first edition of this handbook in 1996, there was little accessible, reliable and methodologically robust guidance available for specifiers seeking to minimise the environmental impacts of building materials. Much of the written information at that time offered only complex numerical assessments that proved difficult for designers and clients to interpret. The first edition of this handbook aimed to provide a simple 'green' guide to the environmental impacts of building materials. Key features of the guide were that it should be both easy to use and soundly based on numerical data.

The *Green Guide* has achieved these aims. The success of the environmental profiling system used is demonstrated by the continuing demand for successive, updated editions. April 2000 saw the release of a version developed specifically to appraise the materials used in housing (*The Green Guide to Housing Specification*, Anderson and Howard, BRE, 2000). Since 1998, the *Green Guide* has been part of BREEAM (BRE Environmental Assessment Method), an accredited environmental rating scheme for buildings. This third edition of the *Green Guide* contains almost 300 specifications, commonly used in all types of building. The profiles included here are based on the latest available industry data. Since the publication of the second edition, information on the relative environmental performance of some materials and components has altered, reflecting both changes in manufacturing practices and our evolving knowledge.

The environmental rankings in this book are based on Life Cycle Assessment studies of environmental impacts. Materials and components are presented in their typical, as-built elemental form. They are compared on a like-for-like basis, for 1 m² of construction, as components that fulfil the same or very similar functions; important variables such as the mass of a material required to fulfil a particular function are therefore taken into account. For example, a direct comparison between the Environmental Profile of 1 tonne of structural steel and 1 tonne of structural concrete would be misleading, as less steel would be required to achieve the same structural performance.

Materials and components are arranged on an elemental basis: external wall construction, internal walls, floor finishes, etc. so that designers and specifiers can compare and select from comparable systems or materials as they compile their specification. Furthermore, it is meaningless to compare the environmental profiles of, say, concrete floors and a particular type of paint; ratings are therefore based only on product performance within each respective element group.

This third edition of the handbook contains an extensive but not complete catalogue of building products. It is intended that the number of products profiled will continue to increase with subsequent editions and that many fixtures, fittings and other components will be added.

Although the environmental ratings in this handbook are underpinned by extensive quantitative data, it was felt that these numerical values and comparisons would be of interest only to specialists rather than those involved in the day-to-day procurement of building projects. These data have therefore been translated into a simple environmental rating system to enable specifiers to make meaningful comparisons between materials and components. As a means to this end, an A, B, C ranking system is used, where 'A' equals least environmental impact/good environmental performance, with B and C ratings increasing in their environmental impact.

The environmental issues considered reflect the generally accepted areas of concern related to the production of building materials used in the UK:

| | |
|---|---|
| Climate change: | Global warming or greenhouse gases |
| Fossil fuel depletion | Coal, oil or gas consumption |
| Ozone depletion | Gases that destroy the ozone layer |
| Human toxicity | Pollutants that are toxic to humans |
| Waste disposal | Material sent to landfill or incineration |
| Water extraction | Mains, surface and groundwater consumption |
| Acid deposition | Gases that cause acid rain, etc. |
| Ecotoxicity | Pollutants that are toxic to the ecosystem |
| Eutrophication | Water pollutants that promote algal blooms, etc. |
| Summer smog | Air pollutants that cause respiratory problems |
| Mineral extraction | Metal ores, minerals and aggregates |

This third edition of the *Green Guide* provides ratings against all these environmental impacts, together with an overall Summary Rating.

By evaluating the performance of materials against these specific environmental parameters, it is possible for the specifier to select materials and components on the basis of personal or organisational preferences or priorities, or take specification decisions based on the performance of a material against a particular environmental parameter.

Perceptions regarding best environmental practice are subject to change as our understanding increases and a clear consensus regarding what is most important and practically achievable emerges. Designers should be aware, for example, of the ongoing debate concerning the merits of recycling and how recycling may not always represent best environmental practice, especially where high-value and polluting energy resources are consumed to recycle low-value material. We have tried to reflect the complexity of this argument to some extent by separately identifying and assessing four key aspects of recycling for the materials within each specification:

- The percentage of recycled material *contained within* a product,
- The percentage *capable of being* recycled
- The percentage *currently being* recycled in the UK, and
- The percentage *saving in embodied energy* if the specification used recycled material rather than virgin.

We would suggest that the merits of recycling should be judged on a case-by-case basis, looking particularly at key issues for each individual material and location. For example, the relatively low impacts of some reclaimed materials can be adversely affected if they have to be transported over very long distances when compared with new materials which may be produced more locally.

The Environmental Profile of a building material is of course only one of many factors to be taken into consideration when compiling a specification; cost, durability, appearance, development control issues, buildability, function, maintenance and availability are all important and potentially decisive issues. The most successful approach to specification is one where underlying objectives and priorities are clearly established in the early stages of a project as this can then help determine the appropriate balance between these sometimes conflicting requirements.

Even in the best buildings, compromise is an inevitable part of design and specification; 'green' considerations will no doubt be subject to this same process of trade-off in achieving the right balance of priorities for a particular project. It is hoped that by thoughtful consideration and the careful use of this book, designers and client organisations will at the very least begin to 'move in the right direction' towards reducing the environmental impacts of construction projects.

## How this edition of *The Green Guide to Specification* relates to other BRE publications and tools

This edition of the *Green Guide* is the latest in a series. Like its predecessor, it can be used within BREEAM to assess the credits for materials specification. It is also one of a suite of tools produced by BRE which provide guidance to designers and specifiers on the environmental impacts of buildings and their construction materials. This chapter explains the history of this edition, and how it relates to other BRE publications and tools.

## *Previous editions of* The Green Guide to Specification

The first edition of *The Green Guide to Specification* was developed by Nigel Howard of Davis Langdon & Everest, and later BRE, and David Shiers of Oxford Brookes University primarily as an in-house publication for what was then The Post Office and their design consultants. Published in 1996 by The Post Office, it was intended to provide guidance on the environmental impacts of common building specifications, including those being considered for use in Post Office properties such as offices, warehouses, sorting offices and for post office branches. Following great interest in the first edition, which had been circulated widely amongst The Post Office's design consultants, a second edition for elements and materials was published by BRE with The Post Office and Oxford Brookes University in September 1998. This version was linked to BREEAM 98 for Offices, the BRE's environmental assessment tool, and was used within BREEAM to assess credits for materials specification.

In order to produce the first two editions of *The Green Guide to Specification*, the authors made use of the best data on the environmental impacts of construction materials available to them at the time. This was adapted where necessary to allow for UK production and electricity generation, differing methodologies, and any perceived bias in studies produced by individual sectoral groups. The recent availability of current, UK-specific information on the environmental impacts associated with construction materials through the BRE Environmental Profiles project, described below, prompted the decision to produce a new edition of the *Green Guide*, to supersede the previous editions.

This new version contains:

- Revised elements and specifications for commercial-scale buildings
- Updated introductory and explanatory text
- New sections covering access and raised floor specifications, hard landscaping and fencing.

## BRE Environmental Profiles of construction materials, components and buildings

In 1999, BRE launched the BRE Environmental Profiles Methodology and Database. This was the culmination of a three-year project funded by the Department of the Environment, Transport and the Regions (DETR) with the partnership of 24 construction manufacturing trade associations. The development and publication of this methodology was a significant achievement, providing the UK with a single agreed approach to the environmental life cycle assessment of all types of construction materials. This methodology received the approval of all the partner trade associations, many of whom provided data on their own manufacturing processes to allow the production of a database of environmental Life Cycle Assessment (LCA) information. Many of these data are now available through the subscription-based BRE Environmental Profiles Database (http://www.bre.co.uk/envprofiles).

Designers and specifiers who are seeking more detailed, numerical LCA data may find the Environmental Profiles database provides them with the information that they require.

Following the publication of the BRE Environmental Profiles Methodology and the resulting availability of UK-specific and current life cycle assessment data, Consignia commissioned BRE and Oxford Brookes to produce this revised guide.

## The Green Guide to Housing Specification

Following the success of using *The Green Guide to Specification* to assess the materials credits within BREEAM 98 for Offices, NHBC sponsored the development of *The Green Guide to Housing Specification* (Anderson and Howard, 2000), to provide equivalent information to the new Eco-Homes Scheme (a version of BREEAM for Homes).

The domestic version works in an identical manner to this edition of the *Green Guide*; however, it specialises in elements and specifications typically used in UK housing construction. The functional units for some elements, for example floor structure, have also been adjusted to reflect the reduced floor loading acceptable for domestic construction.

For designers and specifiers considering their use of materials in most commercial, industrial and medium- to large-scale buildings, this edition of the *Green Guide* is appropriate. However, for small domestic-scale developments, *The Green Guide to Housing Specification* will be more relevant.

## BREEAM

The BRE's Environmental Assessment Method (BREEAM) is a design and management stage assessment tool that provides a credible, transparent, environmental label for buildings based on good practice. One of the aims of BREEAM is to encourage the use of materials that have lower impact on the environment, taking account of the full life cycle of the materials in question.

BREEAM is widely used to specify an overall environmental performance. Its holistic structure means that this approach preserves the design team's flexibility and so maintains their ability to provide overall value through the design process.

Construction materials relate to 10% of the total score available within BREEAM 98 for Offices, making the selection and reuse of materials a significant factor in a building's overall score. The assessment can be applied at the design stage in new build and refurbishment schemes as well as in existing buildings.

There are four credits available within the materials section of a design stage BREEAM assessment for choosing a specified proportion of major building elements that achieve an A Summary Rating in the *Green Guide*. Using the *Green Guide* to assess materials specification in this manner allows BREEAM to address a number of environmental impacts of major building elements, such as embodied energy, emissions, consumption of resources, recycling issues and toxicity in a comprehensive, quick and easy way.

A case study demonstrating how the *Green Guide* can be used to assess a building during a BREEAM assessment is included in Appendix 4. Further information on BREEAM can be found on the BREEAM website http://products.bre.co.uk/breeam.

## Envest

The *Green Guide* is aimed at providing designers and specifiers with the straightforward information they require to produce buildings with lower embodied impacts. Pie charts enable users to gain an idea of the relative importance of different elements in different building types. However, for designers who wish to consider their materials specification in more depth, and understand how their choice of materials relates to the operational impacts of a building (e.g. its heating, lighting and air-conditioning), BRE has developed a software tool called Envest. Intended for use at the initial design stage, Envest allows designers to enter their designs and identify those elements with the most impact. Envest also includes an indication of the operational energy demands to allow designers to investigate the trade-off between the life cycle impacts of their design structure and operational impacts of building use.

Envest is based on much the same data as the *Green Guide*. The majority of the data have been derived from the BRE Environmental Profiles project, and the same weighting system used in the *Green Guide* has been used to produce Ecopoints, the overall measure of environmental impact used in Envest. Further information on Envest is available at www.bre.co.uk/envest.

### *Ecopoints and weightings*

The BRE Environmental Profiles project provides information to users by quantifying the impacts of a material or specification for twelve environmental issues. An experienced user with a background in environmental issues might be able to use this information easily, but for the majority of users within the construction industry, an easier method of dissemination is required. For this reason, BRE developed Ecopoints. A UK Ecopoint is a single score that measures total environmental impact as a proportion of overall impact occurring in the UK. It is calculated by taking the normalised[1] data from the BRE Environmental Profile, applying a weighting factor to each impact and then adding all the weighted impacts to give a total — the Ecopoints.

The weightings have been derived from research funded from the DETR. During 1997/1998, BRE undertook a consensus-based research programme to weight sustainable construction issues. Building on other eco-indicator methods, the study obtained the perspectives of different panels

representing interest groups drawn from across the UK construction industry. These panels assessed economic, social and environmental sustainability issues. Through consultation with the panels, the research established the relative importance of different sustainability issues across the construction industry, finding a significant degree of agreement between the interest groups. The weightings for environmental issues have been used to calculate Ecopoints. It is intended that the weightings will be updated by ongoing research.

The weightings used in Ecopoints are identical to those used to generate the Summary Ratings used in the *Green Guide*. Information on the weightings is provided on pages 12–13, and an example of how Ecopoints and the Summary Ratings are calculated is given in Appendix 2.

## Green procurement

Two important decisions affect the procurement of building products and the building's impact upon the environment:

- *what to buy*, i.e the product type and
- *who to buy it from*.

The *Green Guide* provides assistance to specifiers with the former. It is also useful to distinguish between manufacturers once the type of product has been chosen and this can be achieved in a variety of ways. Certification to ISO 14001 or an eco-management and audit scheme (EMAS) environmental management system can be used as an indicator of good performance by a supplier. Alternatively, evidence of their use of specific measures such as use of raw materials with lower impacts or from local sources or low-emission technologies may also be useful.

Neither an environmental management system nor evidence of a 'single issue' approach to environmental impact will help you to decide how a particular manufacturer's product compares with the typical UK product for the wide range of issues used in the *Green Guide*. Across Europe, many manufacturers are turning to Environmental Declarations to communicate their own environmental performance to their customers. In the UK, the BRE Environmental Profiles scheme provides 'level playing field' declarations, based on the common rules to LCA applied in the *Green Guide*. This scheme allows manufacturers to make claims about their individual product performance as well as allowing trade associations to provide generic information on 'typical UK performance'.

---

[1] 'Normalisation' is the process of making different impacts dimensionless, i.e. without any units, so that they can be added together. In this case, the normalisation factor is the impact of one UK citizen for 1 year. Impacts from a manufacturing process are expressed as a proportion of the same type of impact from one UK citizen.

Specifiers are advised to ask for Environmental Declarations from their suppliers and to use this to satisfy themselves that the company they are using takes a responsible attitude to the management of its environmental performance.

## Life Cycle Assessment

The data at the core of the *Green Guide* are generated using a technique known as Life Cycle Assessment (LCA). LCA is a method of evaluating the environmental impacts of a system taking into account its full life cycle, from the cradle to the grave. This means taking into consideration all the impacts associated with the production and use of a system, from the first time that man has an impact on the environment till the last.

If we take the manufacture and use of a brick wall as an example, then using LCA we would need to consider the environmental impacts associated with:

- the extraction and transport of clay to the brickworks
- the manufacture and transport of ancillary materials
- the extraction and distribution of natural gas for the brick kiln
- the mining and transport of fuels for the generation of electricity for use in the factory
- the production and transport of raw materials for the packaging
- the manufacture and transport of packaging materials for the bricks
- the manufacture of the brick in the brickworks
- the transport of the bricks to the building site
- the extraction of sand and production of cement for the mortar
- the building of the brick wall
- the maintenance of the wall, such as painting or repointing
- the demolition of the wall
- the fate of the materials in the waste stream.

In common with the rest of BRE's sustainable construction tools, this edition of the *Green Guide* uses the BRE Environmental Profiles Methodology as its LCA Methodology. An LCA Methodology is a description of the rules that need to be followed to ensure that the LCA is fair and that the results can be used comparatively. The BRE Environmental Profiles Methodology is compliant with a number of ISO standards (ISO 14040–14043) which have been developed to standardise and define the manner in which life cycle assessments should be undertaken.

One of the most important 'rules' of LCA is the definition of the functional unit. For example, let us say we wanted to compare the environmental impacts of two internal walls — one made of aerated blockwork and one of timber studwork with timber panelling. The BRE Environmental Profiles Database provides data on the environmental impacts associated with the production of a tonne of aerated blockwork and a tonne of UK-consumed kiln-dried softwood in the form of 'per tonne' BRE Environmental Profiles. However, the comparison of the two internal walls cannot be made immediately on the basis of the two profiles. A tonne of each product would produce very different areas of wall. Instead, we need to define the functional unit we will use to compare the two internal walls.

Within the BRE Environmental Profiles Methodology, and therefore in the *Green Guide*, the functional unit is defined as $1\,m^2$ of internal wall, over a 60-year building life. Included in this is any repair and maintenance over the 60-year life, and an assumed dismantling/demolition of the building at the end of its life. Therefore to make the comparison of the two internal walls specifications, we need to calculate the mass of each material needed to produce an average $1\,m^2$ of internal wall, including mortar, plaster and paint (for the aerated blockwork) and timber and paint (for the timber partition). We also need to consider whether any components of the partitions will be repaired or replaced during the 60-year life of the building. For an office building, we will need to take account of 'churn', the regular replacement of partitions as office layouts and tenants change. These 'replacement intervals' have been assigned with advice from BRE's Centre for Whole Life Performance. The final consideration is the fate of the two internal walls when they are replaced or demolished at the end of the building's life. The BRE Environmental Profiles Methodology considers the amount of waste material going to landfill or incineration, and also considers the relative value of any material entering the recycling stream.

For an external wall or roof, the functional unit also takes into account the thermal resistance of the construction, to ensure that all the specifications are compared on a like-for-like basis. Some specifications may use less insulation material (and therefore have a lower initial environmental impact); however, they will also allow much greater heat loss (i.e. operational environmental impact) over the building's lifetime.

An explanation of how environmental impacts are measured and assessed to provide a BRE Environmental Profile for a material using the BRE Environmental Profiles Methodology is included as Appendix 3.

Further information on the BRE Environmental Profiles Methodology can be found on the website (www.bre.co.uk/envprofiles), in the published document by Howard et al. (1999) and in the addendum to the BRE Environmental Profiles Methodology which is available to download from the website.

## Sources of LCA data in *The Green Guide to Specification*

A major source of LCA data for this edition of the *Green Guide* has been the BRE Environmental Profiles Database. The BRE Environmental Profiles Methodology enables environmental assessment of construction materials by using a common 'level playing field' methodology. This allows direct comparison of the environmental impacts of functionally equivalent products. Environmental Profiles produced by BRE using the methodology have been used to assess the following materials within the third edition of *The Green Guide to Specification*:

- Aerated blocks*
- Aggregates (sand and gravel, granite and limestone)**
- Aluminium extrusions and sheet
- Brick**
- Cement**
- Clay roof tiles*
- Concrete roof tiles*
- Dense blocks*
- Galvanised and coated steel sheet**
- Glass wool*
- Ground granulated blast furnace slag*
- Polyurethane foam
- Rock wool*
- Steel reinforcement**
- Structural steel**
- UK-consumed softwood*

* Per tonne Environmental Profiles Data publicly available through the BRE Environmental Profiles Database.
** Environmental Profiles for elemental specifications incorporating these materials publicly available through the BRE Environmental Profiles Database.

BRE Environmental Profiles are the most relevant and representative source of LCA data for the UK construction industry. Wherever permission to use BRE Environmental Profiles has been given by manufacturers, BRE has used these data within this guide. However, some materials have not yet been assessed using the BRE Environmental Profiles Methodology. Where assessment has not occurred, or permission to use BRE Environmental Profiles has not been obtained, BRE has had to refer to other sources of data. These sources include LCA data in the public or private domain and overseas studies, such as the LCA databases compiled by IVAM at the University of Amsterdam, PRé product ecology consultants based in the Netherlands and other well-respected LCA providers. The principal sources are listed in the References at the end of this publication. When necessary, BRE has adapted these studies to take account of differences between UK and overseas practice, in energy mix and in methodology, and improvements in production techniques where older LCA studies have been used. In some cases, data were not available, and have therefore been inferred by analogy or assumption.

In some instances, the use of BRE Environmental Profiles data within this edition compared to the use of older, less representative data within previous editions has had a considerable effect on the performance of some materials and specifications. Users may note, for example, the generally improved performance of aluminium-based specifications in comparison to those in the Second Edition. These used data on aluminium production which did not include the high proportion of recycled content currently used within aluminium components in the construction industry – for example, approximately 70% post-consumer recycled content for aluminium sheet products. They were also based on older studies which did not reflect the improvements in efficiency and pollution control in modern production methods, or the mix of electricity-generating methods used in the countries from which the UK imports the majority of its primary aluminium. The availability of more representative data on aluminium production as a result of the BRE Environmental Profiles project has allowed the ratings for aluminium-based specifications within this edition of the *Green Guide* to more accurately reflect the current situation.

# Environmental Issues

## Climate change

In the UK, nine out of the ten hottest years on record occurred between 1983 and 1998.

Global warming is associated with problems of increased climatic disturbance, rising sea levels, desertification and spread of disease. It has been the subject of major international activity, and methods for measuring it have been presented by the Intergovernmental Panel on Climate Change (IPCC).

Gases recognised as having a 'greenhouse' or global warming effect include CFCs, HCFCs, HFCs, methane and carbon dioxide. Their relative global warming potential (GWP) is calculated by comparing their global warming effect after 100 years to the simultaneous emission of the same mass of carbon dioxide.

## Fossil fuel depletion

UK oil reserves are estimated to provide 33 years' consumption at current rates.

This issue reflects the depletion of the limited resource that fossil fuels represent. It is measured in terms of the primary fossil fuel energy needed for each fuel.

## Ozone depletion

Under EU Regulations, use of CFCs has been banned since January 2001 and HCFCs will no longer be sold after 2010 and will be phased out of use by 2015.

Ozone-depleting gases cause damage to stratospheric ozone or the 'ozone layer'. There is great uncertainty about the combined effects of different gases in the stratosphere and all chlorinated and brominated compounds that are stable enough to reach the stratosphere can have an effect. CFCs, Halons and HCFCs are the major causes of ozone depletion. Damage to the ozone layer reduces its ability to prevent ultraviolet (UV) light entering the earth's atmosphere, increasing the amount of harmful UVB light hitting the earth's surface.

## Human toxicity to air and human toxicity to water[2]

The emission of some substances (such as heavy metals) can have impacts on human health. Assessments of toxicity are based on tolerable concentrations in air, water, air quality guidelines, tolerable daily intake and acceptable daily intake for human toxicity. Impacts to air and water have been combined in the Ratings Tables.

## Ecotoxicity[2]

The emission of some substances such as heavy metals can have impacts on the ecosystem. Assessment of toxicity has been based on maximum tolerable concentrations in water for ecosystems.

## Waste disposal

This issue reflects the depletion of landfill capacity, the noise, dust and odour from landfill (and other disposal) sites, the gaseous emissions and leachate pollution from incineration and landfill, the loss of resources from economic use and risk of underground fires, etc. Insufficient data are available on the fate of materials in landfill or incineration. Instead, a proxy figure for these impacts is measured by tonnes of waste produced.

## Water extraction

This issue is included because of the value of water as a resource and to reflect the depletion, disruption or pollution of aquifers or disruption or pollution of rivers and their ecosystems due to over-extraction.

## Acid deposition

Acidic gases such as sulphur dioxide ($SO_2$) react with water in the atmosphere to form 'acid rain', a process known as acid deposition. When this rain falls, often a considerable distance from the original source of the gas, it causes

---

[2] *Toxicity*: it should be noted that issues relating to toxicity generate much debate. Designers are advised to carefully review the material supplier's guidance, to note any relevant regulations, codes and standards appropriate to different industries and materials and to consider the context and application within which the materials are to be used. The results in the *Green Guide* do consider some toxic effects, but these should in no way be considered comprehensive, for any of the material alternatives considered. Many of the chemicals used in society have not undergone a risk assessment and assessment techniques are still developing.

ecosystem impairment of varying degree, depending upon the nature of the landscape ecosystems. Gases that cause acid deposition include ammonia, hydrochloric acid, hydrogen fluoride, nitrous oxides and sulphur oxides.

## Eutrophication (or 'over-enrichment of water courses')

Nitrates and phosphates are essential for life, but increased concentrations in water can encourage excessive growth of algae, reducing the oxygen within the water. This can lead to increasing mortality of aquatic fauna and flora and to loss of species dependent on low-nutrient environments. Emissions of ammonia, nitrates, nitrogen oxides and phosphorus to air or water all have an impact on eutrophication.

## Summer smog (or 'low-level ozone creation')

Because these reactions depend on sunlight and are common in polluted atmospheres, this issue is known as summer smog.

In atmospheres containing nitrogen oxides (a common pollutant) and volatile organic compounds (VOCs), ozone creation occurs under the influence of radiation from the sun. Different VOCs, such as solvents, methane or petrol, react to form ozone at different rates. Although ozone in the upper part of the atmosphere is essential to prevent ultraviolet light entering the atmosphere, increased ozone in the lower part of the atmosphere is implicated in impacts as diverse as crop damage and increased incidence of asthma and other respiratory complaints.

## Minerals extraction

This issue reflects the total quantity of mineral resource extracted. This applies to all minerals, including metal ore, and applies to both UK and overseas extraction. The extraction of minerals for building in the UK is a high-profile environmental topic, but the minerals themselves are not considered to be scarce. Instead, this issue is a proxy for levels of local environmental impact from mineral extraction such as dust and noise. It assumes that all mineral extractions are equally disruptive of the local environment.

## Embodied energy

Embodied energy is the most frequently cited environmental impact of building materials. For this reason, it may

be a surprise to find that data on this issue are not presented in the *Green Guide*.

Embodied energy is measured using LCA principles, collating information on the total energy used in extraction, manufacture, transport, maintenance and disposal. It is measured in primary rather than delivered terms — in other words it includes the energy used to produce delivered energy — e.g. the energy used to generate electricity or the energy used to mine for coal, as well as the energy in the fuel or power source itself.

If a whole range of processes all use the same sort of energy, for example coal, then the embodied energy for each of these processes provides a good proxy for the amount of climate change or acid rain that each process would cause. However, different processes will use different mixes of fuel and electricity, and many fuels or energy sources can be used to generate electricity. With the Government's target to produce 10% of the UK's electricity from renewable sources by 2010, it is hoped that increasing numbers of manufacturers may move to generating renewable energy for their own processes. As these types of energy have very different environmental impacts from those produced from fossil fuels, then embodied energy will become increasingly less useful as a measure of environmental impact.

To provide a more informative alternative to embodied energy, the BRE Environmental Profiles Methodology uses parameters that reflect the environmental impacts resulting from the *use* of energy:

- The amount of non-renewable resources used in creating the energy for a particular process (measured as *fossil fuel depletion*)
- The amounts of climate change and other pollution caused by the creation of the energy for a particular process (measured as *climate change, acid deposition, summer smog, toxicity*, etc.).

In this way, the real environmental impacts associated with energy use are demonstrated.

The other difficulty of using embodied energy as a proxy for all environmental impacts is that many products can use minimal energy, but still have considerable impacts on the environment — for example in minerals extraction, waste generation and water usage. We therefore believe that the *Green Guide* Summary Rating, based on the BRE weightings and reflecting the twelve environmental issues from the BRE Environmental Profiles, gives a much more accurate picture of overall environmental impact.

## Further information

Further information on these issues, and the way they have been measured and assessed is included in the *BRE Methodology for Environmental Profiles of Construction Materials, Components and Buildings*.

Users may note that these issues have altered from the previous edition. Further information on these changes is presented in Appendix 5.

## How *The Green Guide to Specification* was compiled

### How the elements were chosen

The elements included in this edition of the *Green Guide* cover those parts of the building where the designer or specifier has the opportunity to make a difference to the embodied environmental impact of the building. Elements included range from those, such as external walls, that are fundamental to the appearance of the building, to those, such as the upper floor construction, that are mostly unseen. Some elements, such as floors, are expected to last for the entire life of the building; others, such as suspended ceilings, may be changed regularly through the life of the building.

This edition also contains new elements such as external hard surfacing, boundary protection and sub-structural flooring. With some new office developments providing nine car parking spaces for every ten members of staff, the area of hard surfacing for car parking can be as much as 80% of the floor area, and can add significantly to the embodied environmental impact of the building.

Substructure and superstructure elements have not been included within this edition as it has not been possible to provide either representative functional units for these elements or comparable specifications.

### How the specifications were chosen

Specifications are based on commonly found components, assemblies and materials, modified to reflect the best available data and provide a representative range of specifications. Specifications are based on UK construction practice to satisfy current UK Building Regulations (Spring 2001). Care has been taken to ensure that each specification complies with the functional unit for the element.

### How Green Guide *environmental issue ratings were assessed*

This section provides a brief explanation of how the ratings have been assessed. A worked example providing more detail of the method is included in Appendix 2.

For each specification, the constituent materials, their relative quantities per metre squared and their anticipated life were estimated. The data were analysed over an assumed 60-year building design life. The number of replacements of each component in each specification was calculated by dividing the 60-year period by the replacement interval.

Data on replacement intervals are based on probability of failure or replacement, and the calculation of replacements took account of this by using a factor to allow for the distribution around this replacement interval. The factored number of replacements was then used to multiply the masses of material per metre squared to give a total mass of each material required over the 60-year building life.

The relevant data on the embodied environmental impacts for manufacture of each material used were then collated from sources such as the BRE Environmental Profiles Database. These data were derived for the manufacture of a tonne of each material, and cover the entire process from 'cradle to gate': that is, all the environmental impacts associated with the extraction, processing and transport of raw materials, and the production and manufacturing processes undertaken until the product leaves the factory gate.

Data on environmental impacts from typical transport of materials from the factory gate to site were also produced, based on information provided from the DETR's Continuing Survey of Road Goods Transport.

The fate of 'end-of-life' material arising from replacement and demolition at the end of the 60-year building life was then assessed, and end-of-life profiles for each material covering the associated environmental impacts were produced.

The data on environmental impacts from manufacturing, transport and end of life for each material were then combined with the quantity of each material within each specification over the 60-year life. The sum for each environmental impact for each specification was then calculated, and this was the Environmental Profile for the specification.

In order to calculate the *Green Guide* ratings, the Environmental Profiles for all the specifications within each element group were considered separately. For example, ratings for external walls are assessed separately from the ratings for other elements such as windows. Where necessary for ease of use, element groups have been divided into subsections; for example, 'cavity walls' and 'cladding and masonry' are subsections of external walls. In these cases, all the specifications are still assessed together, irrespective of subsection.

Within each element group, the results for each environmental issue are then compared. For each issue, there will be a range, with the lowest ('minimum') and highest ('maximum') impact identified. The diagram below shows the environmental impacts for seven specifications plotted on the same axis, running from no environmental impact on the left, to high environmental impact on the right.

A, B and C ratings are then calculated for each specification and issue by assessing where the result lies within the range. An 'A' rating is obtained when the result is within the third of the range with the lowest environmental impact, a 'B' rating when it is within the middle third, and a 'C' rating when it is within the third of the range with the highest environmental impact.

## How Green Guide *Summary Ratings are generated*

While some specifiers are happy to make a choice based on their own assessment of the importance of each environmental impact, there is also a demand for a Summary Rating, reflecting overall environmental performance.

The *Green Guide* Summary Rating has been created by adding together the twelve individual impacts. This is made possible using the same approach as for the creation of single-score Ecopoints. Very simply, the issues are treated so that they are measured in common units, weighted for their relative importance and then added together. These summary results were then assigned A, B and C ratings from their position within the range of summary results for each element in exactly the same way as the issue ratings were calculated.

The process of creating common units is an important step because each different impact is measured in a particular unit (e.g. tonnes of waste, kilograms of toxicity) and therefore cannot be added together. The units are 'removed' by a process called normalisation in which the impacts from the life cycle of the specification are divided by the impacts of one UK citizen. The impact for each issue can then be expressed as a relative proportion of one person's impact for one year.

The second step multiplies these dimensionless, normalised data by their respective weighting factor. The derivation of these weighting factors is explained below.

## Weightings

The weighting factors were determined from an extensive BRE research programme which included consultation with representatives from seven different groups, including both

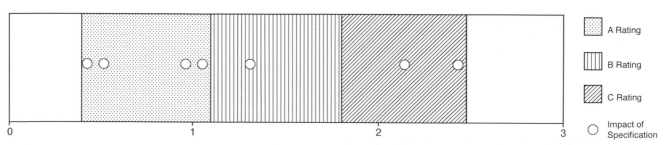

No Environmental Impact  >>>  Low Environmental Impact  >>>  High Environmental Impact (Ecopoints/m²)

How *Green Guide* ratings are assessed

local and central government, materials producers, construction professionals, environmental activists and lobbyists, and academics and researchers. A surprising degree of consensus was found across the groups regarding the relative importance (i.e. weighting) of different environmental issues. From this consensus, it was possible to assign a weight to the different issues covered by the *Green Guide* and hence to derive the Summary Ratings. The environmental issues and their relative weightings are:

| | % |
|---|---|
| Climate change | 38 |
| Fossil fuel depletion | 12 |
| Ozone depletion | 8.2 |
| Human toxicity to air | 7.0 |
| Waste disposal | 6.1 |
| Water extraction | 5.4 |
| Acid deposition | 5.1 |
| Eutrophication | 4.3 |
| Ecotoxicity | 4.3 |
| Summer smog | 3.8 |
| Minerals extraction | 3.5 |
| Human toxicity to water | 2.6 |

## Worked example

To explain how the quantitative LCA data are used to derive the A, B and C ratings for each environmental issue, and how the Summary Rating has been generated, an illustrative worked example has been set out in Appendix 2, based on a loadbearing internal wall.

## Other Issues

Although primarily a 'green' guide, this handbook also provides data on costs, replacement intervals and recycling to ensure that environmental issues are considered within a wider context of specification choices.

## Costs

Indicative as-built costs are provided to assist specifiers in considering environmental issues within the wider context of procurement and project management. Costs are expressed as a range in pounds Sterling per metre squared, and were current at Second Quarter 2001. The costs as shown include materials, labour, plant, overheads and profit and for a level of preliminaries, but do not include allowances for professional fees or VAT. Unlike the environmental issues, the costs are not 'whole life' and do not include allowances for maintenance, repair or replacement over the assumed 60-year life of the building.

The costs stated in this guide are comparative and will be affected by the size, location, market conditions, etc. applicable to any individual project. They should be used for general guidance only.

## Replacement intervals

The specifications within the *Green Guide* are all assessed over a 60-year building life, and they take account of any maintenance, refurbishment or replacement over the building life. Replacement intervals therefore needed to be set for each component or material within each specification. Replacement intervals indicate the typical replacement life of the major components of each element. It should be recognised that these replacement intervals are not always representative of durability, but take account of other factors, such as 'fashion', which may have a greater influence, for example, in the replacement intervals for cladding, or 'churn' (the replacement of, e.g., partitions and carpets with the change of tenants in office accommodation).

Replacement intervals within this edition of the *Green Guide* have been provided by BRE's Centre for Whole Life Performance. This Centre at BRE has considerable expertise in the calculation and assessment of both durability and expected life of components within buildings.

The assumptions made for replacement intervals are given in years for the most frequently replaced major component. For example, for a non-loadbearing timber stud partition, the replacement interval given is 15 years, although the paint has been assumed to be replaced at 5-year intervals. The replacement intervals give an indication of the typical replacement interval — in practice the replacement interval is expected to be distributed around this time period. This distribution is taken into account in the calculation of the *Green Guide* ratings, and further information on how this is done is given in Appendix 2.

The replacement intervals stated in this guide should be used for general guidance only.

## Recycling

The BRE Environmental Profiles Methodology and generated Environmental Profiles already take account of both the *actual* levels of recycled *input*, and the *current* fate of materials at the end of their life cycle, due to the way they are generated. For example, a masonry product made using recycled input will have a reduced mineral extraction impact, and materials such as steel which are recycled are calculated to have lower impact because the LCA methodology passes some of the environmental impacts associated with primary manufacture on to future recycled phases of the materials' life. In the BRE Environmental Profiles Methodology, the proportion transferred is calculated according to the value of primary manufacture relative to recycled manufacture.

However, the authors recognise that specifiers might wish to take account of the *potential* for recycling that exists for construction materials. Specifiers are again reminded of the ongoing debate concerning the merits of recycling and should adhere to best environmental practice when considering waste disposal and use of recycled material. We have tried to reflect the complexity of this argument by separately identifying and assessing four key aspects of recycling for each specification:

1. *Recycled Input:* the percentage (by mass) of recycled or waste material contained within a product;
2. *Recyclability:* the percentage (by mass) of material capable of being recycled or reused at end of life of the product;

3. *Currently recycled:* the percentage (by mass) currently being recycled or reused in the UK;
4. *Energy saved by recycling:* a comparison of the energy required to recycle and/or reuse the specification compared to the energy required to produce similar products from primary resources based on current practice.

The information on recycling has been presented as A, B, C ratings calculated in the same way as those for environmental issues, with an A rating representing good performance.

It is important to note that the A, B, C ratings for recycled input, recyclability, currently recycled and energy saved by recycling do *not* contribute to the *Green Guide* Summary Rating. As explained above, it would be inaccurate to do so. To summarise, this is because the benefits for recycled content and current recycling are already considered quantitatively in the Environmental Profile:

- *Recycled content* is accounted for through lower raw material use and associated impacts and any differences in the efficiency of the manufacturing process.
- *Current recycling* is accounted for by a lower overall impact for the primary manufacturing stage, achieved by passing a proportion of the initial processing on to the recycled material.

# Part II
# How to use *The Green Guide to Specification*

## Layout of the element sections

Each element, e.g. external walls or roofs, has its own section within the *Green Guide*. Some of the elements have been subdivided into particular types of specification for ease of use. For example, the section on the element 'internal walls' has been subdivided into three subsections: (1) loadbearing, (2) non-loadbearing and (3) demountable and proprietary partitions. Further information on how elements have been subdivided is explained in the introduction to each element.

Each section includes:

- A description of the functional unit
- A pie chart indicating the relative importance of the building element in typical building types
- A graph showing the range of A, B and C Summary Ratings for the building element
- A ratings table

## Functional unit

The start of each element section contains information on the functional unit used. A functional unit provides essential information about the general attributes of each specification, including the unit of comparison and its performance characteristics. An example of the functional unit for the upper floor is shown below.

> Functional unit: $1\,m^2$ of upper floor construction, to satisfy building regulations, capable of supporting a live floor load of $2.5\,kN/m^2$ and dead load of $1.85\,kN/m^2$ and including any additional beams to span a 7.5-m column grid. To include any repair, refurbishment or replacement over a 60-year building life.

All the specifications within the element section and, if the element has been subdivided into types of specification, any subsections will have been chosen to comply with the functional unit.

Whilst specifications are generally comparable, there are, inevitably, instances where comparisons are not exactly like for like; e.g. some partitioning systems have load-bearing characteristics whilst others do not. Specifiers are expected to use their expert judgement in such cases.

## Building pie charts

The beginning of most element sections also includes a number of pie charts. These illustrate graphically the contribution that element makes to the total embodied impact of four generic building types over a 60-year building life. The generic building types have been chosen to reflect the common differences between different building types. The pie charts have been built up by assessing a large number of different buildings with different floor plates, number of storeys, and common specifications. In order to highlight the differences between building types and element contributions, the impact of floor finishes (which are normally specified during the building fit-out) has been excluded from the pie charts.

For example, the chart below shows the pie charts for the roofing elements, with the black segment illustrating the percentage of the total building impact relating to roofs for each of the four building types.

A number of uses can be made of the pie charts. Firstly, it can be seen that the impact of roofing varies from around 2% to 10% of the total building impact. It can also be seen that the roof has a greater impact in both the 3-storey buildings than either the 8- or 20-storey buildings. This is as would be expected, as the roof area would be equivalent to

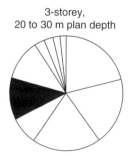

3-storey,
20 to 30 m plan depth

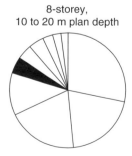

8-storey,
10 to 20 m plan depth

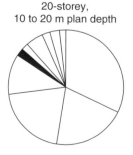

20-storey,
10 to 20 m plan depth

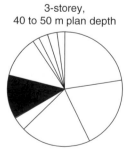

3-storey,
40 to 50 m plan depth

33% of the floor area for a 3-storey building and 5% of the floor area for a 20-storey building. The roof also has slightly more impact for the deeper plan building, reflecting the reduction in external wall and window relative to floor area.

By reviewing the pie chart most closely related to their own building design, users can get an indication of the likely relevance of that element to their own building. Users are advised that the BRE software tool Envest (www.bre.co.uk/envest) allows a much more detailed evaluation of materials specification for particular building designs.

In terms of embodied impact per metre squared, the taller buildings with the deeper floor plans have lower impacts than shorter buildings with narrower floor plans.

## Summary Rating range

The table below shows the summary rating ranges, measured in Ecopoints per metre squared, for all the elements included in the *Green Guide*. As can be seen, the ranges and minimum summary ratings for elements vary considerably.

Floor finishes and roofing elements have the greatest range of Summary Ratings, whilst the range for elements such as internal paint finishes, zero ozone depletion potential (ZODP) insulation and ceiling finishes are much smaller. For elements with a very small range, the difference in impact between an A and a C Summary Rating is obviously much less than for those elements with a large range. Similarly, for elements such as upper floors, where the Summary

Ratings are amongst the highest, the choice of a specification with an A Summary Rating will also have a greater benefit.

Users can also use the ranges to consider the implications of using different elements together — for example, an A-rated upper floor and a C-rated substructural floor system used together can be seen to have a smaller impact than a C-rated upper floor and A-rated substructural floor system. For each element, the table is included with the element Summary Rating range highlighted.

## Significant environmental issues for elements

Using the *Green Guide* data for each element, it is possible to identify the environmental issues that have the greatest significance in determining overall environmental impact. For each element, these are highlighted. C ratings for environmental issues which are listed as significant for the element indicate a greater normalised environmental impact than C ratings for other issues.

## Ratings tables

For each element, the *Green Guide* ratings are displayed in tables. Depending on the number of specifications and whether the element group has been divided into subsections, there may be one or more tables. The layout of the tables is identical in each case — a section from the table on upper floors is included overleaf as an example.

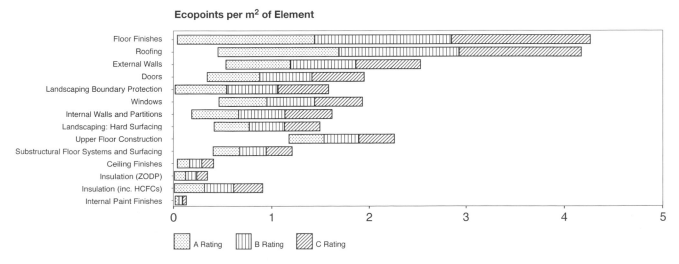

Summary Rating A B C ranges for different elements.

| Element | Summary Rating | Climate Change | Fossil Fuel Depletion | Ozone Depletion | Human Toxicity to Air and Water | Waste Disposal | Water Extraction | Acid Deposition | Ecotoxicity | Eutrophication | Summer Smog | Minerals Extraction | Cost £/m² | Typical Replacement Interval | Recycled Input | Recyclability | Recycled Currently | Energy Saved by Recycling |
|---|---|---|---|---|---|---|---|---|---|---|---|---|---|---|---|---|---|---|
| Beam and blockwork floor with screed | A | A | A | A | A | A | A | A | A | A | A | A | 47-73 | 60 | A | C | C | A |
| Hollow precast reinforced slab and screed | A | A | A | A | A | A | A | A | A | A | A | A | 47-73 | 60 | C | A | C | A |
| Hollow precast reinforced slab with structural topping | B | B | B | A | B | B | B | B | A | B | A | B | 50-80 | 60 | C | A | C | A |

Information on each specification is set out horizontally in rows, starting with a brief description and the Summary Rating. For users wishing to look at a particular environmental issue (or understand how the rating is built up), individual A, B or C ratings for each of the environmental issues are given. Indicative as-built costs follow (current at Second Quarter 2001), expressed as a range in £/m². All costs are inclusive of materials, labour, plant, overheads and profit and for a level of preliminaries, but do not include allowances for professional fees or VAT. The typical replacement interval provides the typical number of years before the replacement of the major components of the specification. Finally, information on recycling relating to the specification is given. As stated, we have tried to reflect the complexity of the issues relating to recycling by separately identifying and assessing four key aspects for each specification.

The information on recycling has been presented as A B C ratings calculated in the same way as those for environmental issues, with an A rating representing good performance within the element group. These ratings do not contribute to the final score.

## Using the ratings

A user looking for a straightforward answer to which specifications within an element group have the lowest environmental impact can review the Summary Ratings for the element group. Those with A ratings will have lower overall environmental impact than those with B ratings, and both will have lower environmental impact than those with C ratings. The Summary Rating takes account of the performance of the specification for each of the environmental issues, and the fact that some issues are assigned more importance than others.

Alternatively, users may compare the different specifications issue by issue and can therefore choose their own weightings for the different environmental issues.

When reviewing ratings, it is important to remember the following points:

- The A B C ratings are only relevant within a specific element group. An A rating in one group is not equivalent to an A rating in another group. Hence, if a user were interested in using cork as insulation, it would not be valid to try to compare the ratings for cork floor tiles (given in the floor finishes section) with those given for corkboard in the insulation materials section.

- The Summary Range graphs show that the A B C Summary Ratings for some elements span a much broader range of values than for other element groups. Hence, in some cases, e.g. internal paint finishes, the A-rated specification may be only slightly better than the C-rated specification, whereas in others, e.g. floor finishes, the difference may be substantial.

- For some environmental issues, the range of values for an element group may be very small, or the values may all be very close to zero, even though A, B and C ratings have been given. Environmental issues with wide ranges or high values are highlighted as significant environmental Issues in the introduction to each element section.

■   The number of A, B and C ratings is not equal for each environmental issue or element. This arises because the spread of results for a range of specifications is rarely evenly distributed within the A, B and C rating subranges. The diagram on page 17 shows how the number of A, B and C ratings depends on how many values lie in each rating range.

■   For borderline cases, products with a similar impact may have different A, B or C ratings. Equally, specifications with the same rating may have quite different levels of impact if one lies at the bottom of a rating range whilst the other lies at the top. In this respect, the Summary Rating is helpful since it is calculated according to the actual performance for each of the parameters.

■   There is no implied weighting between the ratings for different environmental issues. The ratings simply indicate where each specification lies within the range of values found for each group. Only the Summary Rating has been weighted.

■   Most buildings will last much longer (commonly twice as long) than the assumed 60-year design life and hence the value of low maintenance and design for longevity are underestimated in the ratings. For temporary (or short life) buildings these aspects will be overestimated.

■   The ratings are assigned at the time of writing using the best of known available information. It is recognised that our knowledge of these issues is still evolving and the ratings will continue to be updated every 3 to 5 years.

## The importance of different elements

The *Green Guide* enables users to ascertain the relative importance of different elements within their own building design. BRE has calculated the typical embodied environmental impacts relating to a number of generic building models and broken them down into the constituent elements. The contribution of each building element to a typical office building (based on the analysis of a large number of models) is shown as a pie chart below. This includes all the elements of the building, including substructure and superstructure, and covers the maintenance and replacement of elements over the 60-year life.

The pie chart shows that the floor finishes have the greatest impact. A wool/nylon-mix carpet with foam backing/underlay has been chosen as typical for commercial buildings. Because carpets are replaced frequently (perhaps as many as 12 times over a 60-year life), the environmental impacts associated with this element can be very significant – around 40% of the total building impacts. However, changing the specification to a carpet with recycled rubber crumb or natural fibre underlay reduces the overall impact of the floor finishes by up to two-thirds.

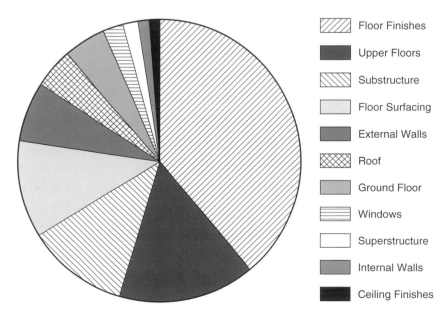

Contribution of building elements to typical building impact

Upper floor structure (forming most of the floor within an office building) has the next largest impact, accounting for around 15% of the total building impacts. Floor surfacing (based on a typical office raised-access floor 150 mm high) is the third largest impact. Raised access floors provide modern offices with considerable flexibility, but at 12% of the total, their environmental impact is significant.

Substructure (foundations, etc.) has a similarly large impact: the specification of substructure is dependent on the ground conditions and the mass of the structure above. The design of substructure may offer designers possibilities of reducing impact, and it is an area that requires further research.

External walls make a significant contribution to the impacts of the typical building (around 7% of the total). Walls and windows together account for 10% of the total embodied impact.

The impacts of the roof and ground floors are of similar magnitude, both around 5% of the building total. The impacts of both roof and ground floor will increase or decrease depending on the number of storeys in the building, the greatest impact being for single-storey buildings.

As with substructure, the design of ground floors (that is floors *in contact* with the ground such as basements) is largely governed by the ground conditions and the choice of substructure. Therefore it is not possible to offer guidance on this.

Of the major design elements, windows have the lowest impact (only 3% of the building total). For a building with higher glazing ratios, the impact of windows will increase as the impact of the external walls reduces.

Superstructure (the structure supporting the floors above ground) has a smaller impact than the other major elements. This conclusion is based on a mix of steel and concrete framed buildings. In fact, the choice of structure makes very little difference to the overall impacts of the building because both account for around 2% of the total.

The smallest impacts (around 1% each for our typical building) are derived from the internal walls (based on a standard open-plan office) and the ceiling finishes (based on a combination of suspended ceiling and plastered soffit options). Although suspended ceilings are likely to be changed relatively frequently over the life of the building, their lightweight nature limits their overall impact.

## Arrangement of the building elements

Materials and components have been arranged into three main groupings within the book:

| | |
|---|---|
| ■ High-mass elements: | Upper floors, external walls and roofs |
| ■ Medium and low-mass elements: | Floor finishes, substructural floors and floor surfacing, windows, internal walls, ceilings and doors |
| ■ Other materials and elements: | Paint systems, insulation and landscaping. |

Typically, the upper floors, external walls and roof of a 4-storey building can account for 45% of the total building mass, with a further 40% contained within the substructure and ground floor. This is mirrored by environmental impacts — the upper floors, external walls and roof have over 25% of the impact of a typical building over 60 years, and a further 15% arises from the substructure and ground floor.

Floor finishes (which are frequently replaced) and substructural floors and floor surfacing are low- and medium-mass elements which have a significant impact. Carpeting represents just under 40% of the typical building's impact and the raised access floor represents just over 10%.

Whilst all specification choices are important, designers may wish to give particular attention to the elements of the building with the greatest environmental impact:

■ floor construction, floor surfacing and floor finishes
■ external walls and windows
■ roofs.

# Part III
# *Green Guide* ratings

# High-mass elements

# Upper floors

Functional Unit: 1 m² of upper floor construction, to satisfy Building Regulations, capable of supporting a live floor load of 2.5 kN/m² and dead load of 1.85 kN/m² and including any additional beams to span a 7.5-m column grid. To include any repair, refurbishment or replacement over a 60-year building life.

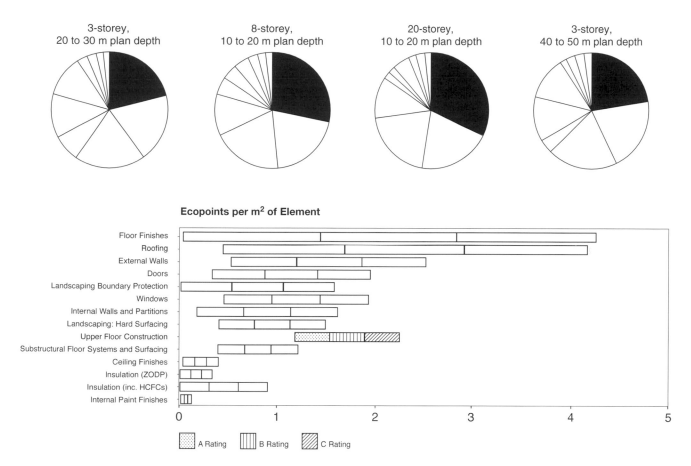

Summary Rating A B C ranges for different elements.

## Significant environmental issues for this element

Climate change, minerals extraction and waste disposal.

In order to highlight the differences between building types and element contributions, the impact of floor finishes (which are normally specified during the building fit-out and generally have the largest impact) have been excluded from the pie charts. These show that upper floor construction makes the largest contribution to the overall building impact for each of the building types, a finding that draws a parallel to the significant contribution of upper floors to the total building mass. As would be expected for this type of construction, the significant environmental impacts largely relate to the use of minerals and the disposal impacts after demolition.

The impact of upper floors increases appreciably with the increase in the number of storeys in the building, as the impacts of the roof and ground floors become less important; thus the impact is smallest for the two 3-storey buildings.

This section on upper floors applies to all floor constructions that are not in contact with the ground. This includes floors to be constructed at ground level, but above a basement.

## BREEAM

One credit is available in BREEAM for the use of A-rated specifications for over 80% (by area) of the upper floors. Appendix 4 provides further information on BREEAM assessment.

# Upper Floors

| Element | Summary Rating | Climate Change | Fossil Fuel Depletion | Ozone Depletion | Human Toxicity to Air and Water | Waste Disposal | Water Extraction | Acid Deposition | Ecotoxicity | Eutrophication | Summer Smog | Minerals Extraction | Cost £/m² | Typical Replacement Interval | Recycled Input | Recyclability | Recycled Currently | Energy Saved by Recycling |
|---|---|---|---|---|---|---|---|---|---|---|---|---|---|---|---|---|---|---|
| Beam and blockwork floor with screed | A | A | A | A | A | A | A | A | A | A | A | A | 47-73 | 60 | A | C | C | A |
| Hollow precast reinforced slab and screed | A | A | A | A | A | A | A | A | A | A | A | A | 47-73 | 60 | C | A | C | A |
| Hollow precast reinforced slab with structural topping | B | B | B | A | B | B | B | B | A | B | A | B | 50-80 | 60 | C | A | C | A |
| In situ reinforced concrete slab | C | B | B | A | B | C | B | B | A | B | A | C | 40-60 | 60 | C | A | C | A |
| In situ reinforced concrete trough slab | B | A | A | A | A | B | A | A | A | A | A | B | 40-60 | 60 | C | A | C | A |
| In situ reinforced concrete waffle slab | B | A | A | A | A | B | A | A | A | A | A | B | 40-60 | 60 | C | A | C | A |
| Lattice girder precast concrete floor with in situ concrete topping | B | A | A | A | B | B | A | A | A | A | A | C | 84-153 | 60 | C | A | C | A |
| Lattice girder precast concrete floor with polystyrene void formers and in situ concrete topping | B | B | C | A | A | A | A | B | A | A | A | A | 84-153 | 60 | C | B | C | C |
| Profiled steel permanent steel shuttering, in-situ concrete slab, steel reinforcement bars and mesh | B | B | C | A | A | B | C | A | C | A | C | B | 55-120 | 60 | C | A | A | A |
| Solid prestressed composite floor with structural topping | C | C | C | A | C | C | C | C | A | C | A | C | 65-90 | 60 | C | A | C | A |

The previous edition of the *Green Guide* included a number of timber floor specifications which would not have satisfied the functional unit used within this edition — particularly in relation to the span and loading. In general, timber floors, i.e. boards on timber joists, perform significantly better than the specifications above. For designers and specifiers wishing to obtain more detailed guidance on flooring options for more domestic-scale construction (including timber floors), *The Green Guide to Housing Specification* rates a wide range of floor specifications designed for smaller spans and floor loadings.

For most commercial applications, concrete floors are the only viable option. Precast units can often substantially reduce the mass of the floor structure whilst maintaining high floor loadings. Systems using hollow or lightweight components are likely to give the best environmental option. High mass concrete floors are the poorest performers in environmental terms. For similar floor types satisfying the same load and span characteristics, floors using a structural topping are significantly heavier per metre squared and so perform less well.

The use of pulverised fuel ash (PFA or fly ash) and ground granulated blastfurnace slag (GGBS) within concrete is widespread, accounting for over 10% of the UK cement market. As relatively low-value by-products from other industrial processes (electricity and steel production), they have small environmental impacts and their use in concrete and as aggregate has significant benefit in decreasing its embodied environmental impacts.

The extraction of virgin aggregate has significant impacts on the landscape and communities around quarries, and the use of recycled aggregate (in this context, crushed concrete or similar) should therefore be encouraged. However, in energy terms, the crushing, sorting and transport of recycled aggregate has very similar impacts to the quarrying, sorting and transport of virgin aggregate. There may be quality control and material performance issues that need to be addressed when using recycled aggregate, i.e. where the size and constituents of aggregates are important in determining the strength and integrity of a structural element. The availability of high-quality recycled material is increasing rapidly, but where concerns about its quality result in the specification of higher cement content, the benefits of using recycled aggregate in concrete can be lost. For this reason, greater benefit may be gained through the use of recycled aggregates as fill or hardcore.

## Ground floors and substructure

Although ground floor construction is not included as a separate section in this guide, the information given on upper floors reveals a number of key principles that could also be applied to ground floor construction. Suspended timber floors would usually be the preferred environmental option for ground floor construction, but are rarely structurally practical for commercial applications. Beam and blockwork floors, now commonly used in a range of building types, for reasons of speed on site, quality control and the avoidance of the effects of ground movement, would also be a good environmental option due to their relatively low mass. Further guidance on more domestic-scale ground floor construction can be found in *The Green Guide to Housing Specification*.

Cellar and basement construction can contribute significantly to an environmental profile of a building. This is due to the high mass of the materials needed to withstand both high levels of lateral loading (from the ground and water) and the vertical loads imposed by the building. Although concrete is a very low embodied energy material, it needs to be used in high mass underground and its use needs to be carefully considered.

## Insulation

For ground floor/basement construction, the choice of insulation is often determined on the basis of resistance to moisture and/or loading rather than thermal performance. Specifiers should refer to the section on insulation in Appendix 1 for further information. As in the case of wall and roof insulation, the small mass of insulation needed to satisfy Building Regulation requirements means that compared with the mass of the materials used in the rest of the floor construction, the impacts of the floor construction would not be sensitive to the type of insulation chosen, as long as the insulation is not ozone-depleting.

# External walls

Functional unit: 1 m² of external wall construction, to satisfy current Building Regulations, but to satisfy a U value of 0.35 W/m²K to reflect the proposed revision to Part L currently in consultation. Where relevant, the specification will also include an internal wall finish, for example painted plaster. To include any repair, refurbishment or replacement over a 60-year building life.

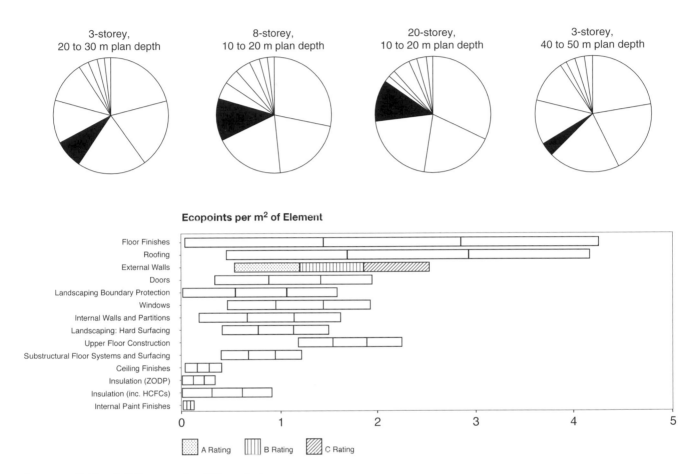

Summary Rating A B C ranges for different elements.

## Significant environmental issues for this element

Climate change, acidification, fossil fuel depletion, minerals extraction and waste disposal.

Perhaps more than any other decision facing the designer, the choice of the external wall specification is subject to the widest range of practical, economic and visual considerations, some of which may be beyond the control or influence of the design team. Client requirements or preferences and development control issues may largely determine the building form and the choice of external materials and designers may therefore find themselves in a position where choice is limited and environmental compromise inevitable.

The external envelope is also the key factor in portraying the character and design philosophy of the building because this is the building's 'public face'. Once established, compromise in the designer's original vision of the building may be strongly resisted. For this reason, it is important that designers should not regard environmental considerations as 'bolt-on' extras to the building design. With careful thought at the outset of projects, building design can (and should) take a holistic and integrated approach incorporating technical, cost and environmental considerations into the design strategy. The degree to which each of these aspects is prioritised or compromised should flow from a clearly established project philosophy agreed by the design team and client organisation at the outset and will vary project-to-project.

The pie charts show that the external walls can have a significant contribution to the impacts of the building. In a typical 4-storey office building, the external wall can account for around 20% of the building's mass above ground. The external wall can also account for around 30% of building costs, so designers should consider the benefits of minimising the external wall area for a given plan area by avoiding long and narrow or complex plan forms which have a high wall to floor ratio. Simple plan forms with a relatively low external wall area and maximum floor space will benefit the project in terms of capital cost, running cost (lower maintenance and heat loss) and environmental impact. This reduction in environmental impact is echoed in the pie charts, with the external walls of the deeper plan buildings having a much lower contribution to the overall building impact than for the two narrower plan buildings.

External wall specifications include a diverse range of construction types and materials; it is therefore no surprise that a wide range of environmental issues are significant for this element.

## Superstructure

Structural columns within frames and the primary structural elements within loadbearing construction have not been taken into account in the profiles. Secondary structure such as cladding rails has been included. Inclusion of primary structure would have become overly complex due to the many variables and alternative structural solutions of framed construction design. Moreover, the majority of the structural mass in framed buildings is associated with the support of floors rather than of the external walls and so would make little difference to estimates of overall mass and consequent environmental profile.

## General comments on external walls

As a general principle, the lower the mass of materials and the less they are the product of resource- and energy-intensive manufacturing processes, the more favourable the environmental profile. Hence, for wall construction, the profiling results show the benefits of timber framing and low-mass construction. However, traditional brickwork cavity wall construction also performs well, particularly if used with an aerated blockwork inner leaf. Aluminium systems are amongst the lowest impact specifications and show improved environmental performance when compared with previous editions of the *Green Guide*. As stated, these used data on aluminium production that did not

include the high proportion of recycled content currently used within aluminium components in the construction industry — over 70% for aluminium sheet products. They were also based on older studies which did not reflect the improvements in modern production methods, or the mix of electricity generating methods used in the countries from which the UK imports the majority of its primary aluminium. The availability of more representative data on aluminium production as a result of the BRE Environmental Profiles project has allowed the ratings within this edition of the *Green Guide* to more accurately reflect the current situation.

The evaluation of the coated steel and aluminium used in these specifications takes account of the mix of coatings, such as powder coating, polyester or plastisol normally used. Compared with the impact of the other components in these specifications, the impact of the coatings is small due to their very small mass. Steel panels without coatings would be expected to have a shorter life and therefore significantly higher impact.

## Insulation

It is important to refer to the section on insulation materials in Appendix 1 when considering the specification of external walls. Due to the relatively small proportion of insulation materials in the mass required in external walls, the ratings shown here are not generally affected by the type of insulation chosen. The exception to this, however, would be if insulating materials were chosen that used ozone-depleting chemicals such as HCFCs. In such circumstances, the resulting increased climate change and ozone-depletion impacts would affect the Summary Ratings for external walls by one increment, so that an 'A' Summary Rating would become a 'B', a 'B' would move to a 'C' and a 'C' would be so adversely affected as to move it into a 'sub-category'[3].

## BREEAM

One credit is available in BREEAM for the use of A-rated specifications for over 80% (by area) of the external walls.

[3] When used in a BREEAM assessment, this incremental change in rating is accomplished through the loss of a credit which is awarded to those buildings where the specification of insulates avoids the use of ozone-depleting substances in either manufacture or composition. For further details see Appendix 4.

Appendix 4 provides further information on BREEAM assessment.

## Division of external wall specifications into subsections

External wall specifications have been arranged into four generic groupings in order to make access to information easier. However, ratings are based on comparative performance across *all* the options set out below:

- Traditional forms of cavity wall construction
- 'Rainscreen' claddings — weatherboarding, tile-hung, etc.
- Cladding and masonry construction
- Cladding and framed construction, including 'industrial shed' specifications

The clear-glazed areas of curtain walling systems do not satisfy the external walling functional unit as they do not offer enough thermal resistance — they have therefore been included as window elements. If an aluminium-framed glazed curtain walling system had been assessed within the external wall section and the impacts of additional heating and cooling energy for the building were ignored, it would have achieved a B Summary Rating.

# Traditional forms of cavity wall construction

| Element | Summary Rating | Climate Change | Fossil Fuel Depletion | Ozone Depletion | Human Toxicity to Air and Water | Waste Disposal | Water Extraction | Acid Deposition | Ecotoxicity | Eutrophication | Summer Smog | Minerals Extraction | Cost £/m² | Typical Replacement Interval | Recycled Input | Recyclability | Recycled Currently | Energy Saved by Recycling |
|---|---|---|---|---|---|---|---|---|---|---|---|---|---|---|---|---|---|---|
| Brickwork outer leaf, insulation, aerated blockwork inner leaf, plasterboard/plaster | A | A | A | A | A | B | A | A | A | A | A | A | 55-105 | 60 | C | A | B | A |
| Brickwork outer leaf, insulation, dense blockwork inner leaf, plasterboard/plaster | A | A | A | A | A | C | A | A | A | A | A | A | 55-105 | 60 | C | A | B | A |
| Brickwork, timber frame with insulation, plasterboard | A | A | A | A | A | B | A | A | A | A | A | A | 60-97 | 60 | C | A | B | A |
| Fairfaced reconstituted stone outer leaf, insulation, dense blockwork inner leaf, plasterboard/plaster | B | A | A | A | A | C | A | A | C | B | A | B | 125-150 | 60 | C | A | B | A |
| Natural stone outer leaf, insulation, dense blockwork inner leaf, plasterboard/plaster | A | A | A | A | A | C | A | A | C | B | A | B | 576-761 | 60 | C | A | A | B |
| Rendered dense blockwork outer leaf, insulation, dense blockwork inner leaf, plasterboard/plaster | A | A | A | A | A | C | A | A | A | A | A | A | 63-81 | 60 | C | A | B | A |
| Rendered dense blockwork outer leaf, insulation, aerated blockwork inner leaf, plasterboard/plaster | A | A | A | A | A | C | A | A | A | A | A | A | 63-81 | 60 | C | A | B | A |

Natural stone with a blockwork inner leaf provides a heavyweight construction of good environmental performance. This is primarily because stone is a minimally processed material. Designers and specifiers may wish to satisfy themselves that the source of the stone — the quarries — are being responsibly managed in terms of their environmental impact and future use. This result is derived assuming a UK-produced stone with average transport distances; stone travelling very long distances by road would not perform so well.

In previous studies, brickwork has been found to perform less well than other masonry options, because of the energy required to fire the brick. However, changes in manufacturing processes and the availability of new data from manufacturers where continuous kilning is standard practice (energy use therefore being less than in processes where kilns are allowed to cool between production batches) are showing the typically produced UK brick to have

comparably low, 'A'-rated environmental impacts compared to other masonry alternatives. Specifiers should be aware that handmade or intermittently kilned bricks will have significantly more impact than their continuously kilned, machine-made counterparts.

Brickwork is also likely to provide an effective life (often over 100 years) far exceeding the scope of consideration of this project (60 years); brick construction may indeed last many hundreds of years. Bricks also have good recyclability attributes if used with easily removable lime mortars. Where such mortars are not used, brickwork and indeed the majority of the other masonry options can only be recycled into lower grade 'fill'. Reclaimed bricks can, of course, be utilised in masonry wall construction and are available in most areas of the UK and they would have lower environmental impact than new bricks.

The single timber-framed specification performs very well,

achieving an 'A' rating due to the low-energy nature of the materials in the specification.

Although showing the same A B C ratings as natural stone for each environmental issue, the reconstituted stone specification was the worst performing material in this subsection. It scores a B rating because it performs worse within the range for each issue category. Generally, this poorer performance was due to the requirement for more intensive, higher energy production processes.

Rendered blockwork performs as well as brick cavity wall construction, due to low energy use and consequently lower emissions. Maintenance requirements may place a greater long-term burden on building owners.

# 'Rainscreen' claddings

| Element | Summary Rating | Climate Change | Fossil Fuel Depletion | Ozone Depletion | Human Toxicity to Air and Water | Waste Disposal | Water Extraction | Acid Deposition | Ecotoxicity | Eutrophication | Summer Smog | Minerals Extraction | Cost £/m² | Typical Replacement Interval | Recycled Input | Recyclability | Recycled Currently | Energy Saved by Recycling |
|---|---|---|---|---|---|---|---|---|---|---|---|---|---|---|---|---|---|---|
| Clay tiles, battens, insulation, dense blockwork, plasterboard/plaster | A | A | A | A | A | B | A | A | A | A | A | A | 74-80 | 40 | C | A | B | A |
| Concrete tiles, battens, insulation, dense blockwork, plasterboard/plaster | A | A | A | A | A | B | A | A | A | A | A | A | 68-74 | 40 | C | A | B | A |
| PVC-u weatherboarding, insulation, dense blockwork, plasterboard/plaster | C | C | C | A | C | B | A | C | C | A | A | A | 70-80 | 25 | C | B | B | C |
| Terracotta rainscreen cladding, aluminium framework, expanded polystyrene insulation, dense blockwork, plasterboard/plaster | B | B | B | A | A | B | A | B | A | A | A | A | 95-110 | 40 | C | A | B | A |
| Treated softwood weatherboarding, insulation, dense blockwork, plasterboard/plaster | A | A | A | A | A | B | A | A | A | A | B | A | 60-69 | 30 | C | A | B | A |
| Western Red Cedar cladding on timber framework, insulation, dense blockwork, plasterboard/plaster | A | A | A | A | A | B | A | A | A | A | A | A | 64-75 | 40 | C | C | C | B |

Of the six specifications profiled in this subsection, the best performers are the clay tile, the concrete tile, the softwood weatherboarding and the Western Red Cedar cladding. Western Red Cedar is generally considered to be a 'low-maintenance' material and, as such, represents an attractive option both in terms of economic and environmental performance.

Designers should be aware that some imported timbers used for timber weatherboarding, although transported in part by sea (a very environmentally efficient method of transporting freight compared with road transport), are often moved across or between countries by road. This can result in some timbers having a high environmental impact from freight transport. Important caveats apply to the selection of timber; further information on the responsible specification of timber is included in Appendix 1.

# Cladding and masonry construction

| Element | Summary Rating | Climate Change | Fossil Fuel Depletion | Ozone Depletion | Human Toxicity to Air and Water | Waste Disposal | Water Extraction | Acid Deposition | Ecotoxicity | Eutrophication | Summer Smog | Minerals Extraction | Cost £/m² | Typical Replacement Interval | Recycled Input | Recyclability | Recycled Currently | Energy Saved by Recycling |
|---|---|---|---|---|---|---|---|---|---|---|---|---|---|---|---|---|---|---|
| Aluminium insulated composite cladding panel, galvanised steel fixing rail, aerated blockwork, plasterboard/plaster | A | B | A | A | A | A | A | A | A | A | B | A | 52-80 | 25 | A | A | A | A |
| Aluminium insulated composite cladding panel, galvanised steel fixing rail, dense blockwork (140 mm), plasterboard/plaster | B | B | A | A | B | B | B | A | A | B | B | A | 54-82 | 25 | C | A | B | A |
| Aluminium insulated composite cladding panel, galvanised steel fixing rails, dense blockwork, plasterboard/plaster | A | A | A | A | A | B | A | A | A | A | A | A | 69-99 | 25 | C | A | B | A |
| Aluminium profiled single skin cladding, insulation, galvanised steel fixing rails, aerated blockwork, plasterboard/plaster | A | A | A | A | A | A | A | A | A | A | A | A | 81-117 | 25 | A | B | B | A |
| Aluminium profiled single skin cladding, insulation, galvanised steel fixing rails, dense blockwork (140 mm), plasterboard/plaster | A | A | A | A | A | B | A | A | A | A | A | A | 88-123 | 25 | C | A | B | A |
| Aluminium profiled single skin cladding, insulation, galvanised steel fixing rails, dense blockwork, plasterboard/plaster | A | A | A | A | A | B | A | A | A | A | A | A | 81-117 | 25 | C | A | B | A |
| Aluminium profiled single skin cladding, insulation, galvanised steel fixing rails, precast concrete panel, plasterboard/plaster | B | B | A | A | B | B | A | A | A | A | A | B | 162-238 | 25 | C | A | B | A |
| Coated steel insulated composite cladding panel, galvanised steel fixing rail, aerated blockwork, plasterboard/plaster | B | B | B | A | A | A | B | A | A | A | B | A | 82-112 | 25 | B | A | A | A |
| Coated steel insulated composite cladding panel, galvanised steel fixing rail, dense blockwork, plasterboard/plaster | B | B | B | A | A | B | B | A | A | B | B | A | 82-112 | 25 | C | A | A | A |
| Coated steel profiled single skin cladding, insulation, galvanised steel fixing rails, aerated blockwork, plasterboard/plaster | A | A | A | A | A | A | A | A | A | A | A | A | 67-97 | 25 | A | B | B | A |
| Coated steel profiled single skin cladding, insulation, galvanised steel fixing rails, dense blockwork (140 mm), plasterboard/plaster | A | A | A | A | A | B | A | A | A | A | A | A | 73-103 | 25 | C | A | B | A |
| Coated steel profiled single skin cladding, insulation, galvanised steel fixing rails, dense blockwork, plasterboard/plaster | A | A | A | A | A | B | A | A | A | A | A | A | 67-97 | 25 | C | A | B | B |

*Continued*

| Element | Summary Rating | Climate Change | Fossil Fuel Depletion | Ozone Depletion | Human Toxicity to Air and Water | Waste Disposal | Water Extraction | Acid Deposition | Ecotoxicity | Eutrophication | Summer Smog | Minerals Extraction | Cost £/m² | Typical Replacement Interval | Recycled Input | Recyclability | Recycled Currently | Energy Saved by Recycling |
|---|---|---|---|---|---|---|---|---|---|---|---|---|---|---|---|---|---|---|
| Coated steel profiled single skin cladding, insulation, galvanised steel fixing rails, precast concrete panel, plasterboard/plaster | B | A | A | A | A | B | A | A | A | A | A | B | 153-246 | 25 | C | A | B | A |
| Glass reinforced plastic (GRP) cladding, aluminium fixing rails, insulation, aerated blockwork, plasterboard/plaster | A | B | A | A | B | A | A | A | A | A | A | A | 163-173 | 25 | A | B | B | A |
| Glass reinforced plastic (GRP) cladding, aluminium fixing rails, insulation, dense blockwork, plasterboard/plaster | B | B | A | A | B | B | A | A | A | A | A | A | 163-173 | 25 | C | A | B | A |
| Marble cladding, insulation, dense blockwork, plasterboard/plaster | B | B | A | A | B | C | A | A | C | B | A | B | 194-517 | 25 | C | A | A | A |
| Marble cladding, insulation, precast concrete panel, plasterboard/plaster | C | B | A | A | C | C | A | B | C | C | A | C | 280-670 | 25 | C | A | A | A |
| Polymeric render with glass wool reinforcement on insulation on aerated blockwork, plasterboard | B | C | C | A | A | A | A | C | B | A | A | A | 55-65 | 20 | A | C | C | C |
| Polymeric render with glass wool reinforcement on insulation on dense blockwork, plasterboard | B | C | C | A | A | B | A | C | B | A | A | A | 55-65 | 20 | C | B | B | C |
| Polymeric render, glass wool mesh, insulation, precast concrete panels, plasterboard/plaster | C | C | C | A | B | B | A | C | B | B | A | B | 160-235 | 20 | C | A | B | C |
| Precast concrete cladding, insulation, dense blockwork (140 mm), plasterboard/plaster | B | A | A | A | A | C | A | A | A | B | A | B | 127-194 | 40 | C | A | B | A |
| Precast concrete cladding, insulation, aerated blockwork, plasterboard/plaster | B | A | A | A | A | B | A | A | A | A | A | B | 120-188 | 40 | C | A | B | A |
| Precast concrete cladding, insulation, dense blockwork, plasterboard/plaster | B | A | A | A | A | C | A | A | A | A | A | B | 120-188 | 40 | C | A | B | A |
| Precast concrete cladding, insulation, precast concrete panel, plasterboard/plaster | B | B | A | A | B | C | A | A | A | B | A | C | 206-337 | 40 | C | A | B | A |
| Stainless steel cladding and coated steel lining panel, galvanised steel fixing rail, insulation, dense blockwork, plasterboard/plaster | A | A | A | A | A | B | A | A | A | A | B | A | 106-144 | 40 | C | A | B | A |
| Stainless steel profiled cladding, insulation, galvanised steel fixing rails, dense blockwork (140 mm), plasterboard/plaster | A | A | A | A | A | B | A | A | A | A | A | A | 80-107 | 40 | C | A | B | A |

The choice of masonry affects the overall impact — specifications using the precast concrete panels have greater impacts, and thicker blockwork specifications can affect the Summary Rating. The composite cladding panels have greater impact than the profiled single skin cladding as almost double the amount of metal is required.

The poorest performers are the marble cladding and the polymeric renders. Although a natural material, the marble cladding is a very high-mass/high-density material used in thick panel form and requires considerable support. The resins used in polymeric renders require higher levels of energy and oil feedstock in their manufacture which contributes to their greater impact.

# Cladding and framed construction

| Element | Summary Rating | Climate Change | Fossil Fuel Depletion | Ozone Depletion | Human Toxicity to Air and Water | Waste Disposal | Water Extraction | Acid Deposition | Ecotoxicity | Eutrophication | Summer Smog | Minerals Extraction | Cost £/m² | Typical Replacement Interval | Recycled Input | Recyclability | Recycled Currently | Energy Saved by Recycling |
|---|---|---|---|---|---|---|---|---|---|---|---|---|---|---|---|---|---|---|
| Aluminium framed opaque insulated glazed curtain walling system | C | C | B | A | C | A | A | B | B | C | A | A | 500-650 | 25 | C | A | C | B |
| Aluminium insulated composite cladding panels, galvanised steel fixing rail, plasterboard on steel stud | B | B | B | A | B | A | B | A | A | B | C | A | 36-61 | 25 | C | B | A | A |
| Aluminium profiled double skin cladding, insulation, galvanised steel fixing rails, plasterboard internal wall on steel stud | B | B | B | A | A | A | B | A | A | A | B | A | 50-78 | 25 | B | B | A | A |
| Coated steel insulated composite cladding panel, galvanised steel fixing rail, insulation, plasterboard internal wall on steel stud | B | C | B | A | A | A | C | A | A | B | C | A | 63-91 | 25 | C | B | A | A |
| Coated steel insulated composite cladding with aluminium lining panel, galvanised steel fixing rail, plasterboard on steel stud | B | C | B | A | B | A | C | A | A | B | C | A | 63-91 | 25 | C | B | A | A |
| Coated steel profiled double skin cladding, galvanised steel fixing rails, insulation, plasterboard internal wall on steel stud | B | C | B | A | A | A | C | A | A | B | C | A | 65-93 | 25 | C | B | A | A |
| Glass reinforced plastic (GRP) cladding, aluminium fixing rails, insulation, plasterboard internal wall on steel stud | B | B | B | A | B | A | A | B | A | B | B | A | 147-154 | 25 | B | C | B | A |
| Precast concrete cladding, stainless steel fixing rails, insulation, plasterboard on steel stud | B | B | A | A | A | B | B | A | A | B | B | B | 103-169 | 40 | C | A | B | A |
| Stainless steel cladding and coated steel lining panel, galvanised steel fixing rail, insulation, plasterboard internal wall on steel stud | A | B | A | A | A | A | B | A | A | A | B | A | 99-134 | 40 | B | B | A | B |
| **'INDUSTRIAL SHED' SPECIFICATIONS** | | | | | | | | | | | | | | | | | | |
| Aluminium profiled double skin cladding, galvanised steel fixing rail, insulation | A | B | A | A | A | A | A | A | A | A | B | A | 24-48 | 25 | B | A | A | A |
| Coated steel insulated composite cladding panels | A | B | A | A | A | A | B | A | A | A | B | A | 38-64 | 25 | C | A | A | A |
| Coated steel profiled double skin cladding, galvanised steel fixing rail, insulation | A | A | A | A | A | A | B | A | A | A | B | A | 65-93 | 25 | C | A | A | A |
| Aluminium insulated composite cladding panels | A | B | A | A | A | A | A | A | A | A | B | A | 36-63 | 25 | B | A | A | A |
| Stainless steel profiled cladding with coated steel inner skin, galvanised steel fixing rails, insulation | A | A | A | A | A | A | A | A | A | A | A | A | 90-125 | 25 | A | A | A | B |

The best-performing specifications in this subsection are the stainless steel cladding and 'industrial shed' specifications. Stainless steel cladding profiles extremely well, combining the benefits of lightweight cladding together with good recycling attributes — most production worldwide now comes from recycled steel feedstocks — and consequently gives relatively low embodied energy and pollutant emissions.

Of the other wall cladding systems, most perform only intermediately, scoring 'B' ratings.

# Roofs

Functional unit: 1 m² of roof construction, measured horizontally, to satisfy Building Regulations, in particular a U value of 0.25 W/m²K. To include any repair, refurbishment or replacement over a 60-year building life.

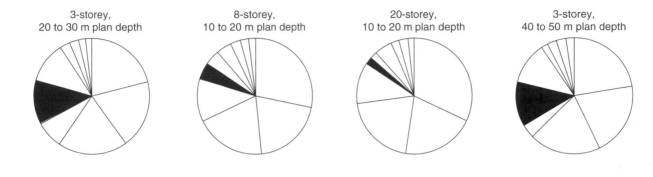

3-storey, 20 to 30 m plan depth | 8-storey, 10 to 20 m plan depth | 20-storey, 10 to 20 m plan depth | 3-storey, 40 to 50 m plan depth

**Ecopoints per m² of Element**

- Floor Finishes
- Roofing
- External Walls
- Doors
- Landscaping Boundary Protection
- Windows
- Internal Walls and Partitions
- Landscaping: Hard Surfacing
- Upper Floor Construction
- Substructural Floor Systems and Surfacing
- Ceiling Finishes
- Insulation (ZODP)
- Insulation (inc. HCFCs)
- Internal Paint Finishes

A Rating    B Rating    C Rating

Summary Rating A B C ranges for different elements.

## Significant environmental issues for this element

Climate change, acidification, fossil fuel depletion, minerals extraction and waste disposal

The pie charts show that for the four building models, the roof's contribution to the building's impact varies from around 2% to 12%. It can be seen that the roof has greater impact for both of the 3-storey buildings in comparison to either the 8- or 20-storey buildings. This is as would be expected, as the roof area would be equivalent to 33% of the floor area for a 3-storey building and only 5% of the floor area for a 20-storey building. The roof also has slightly more impact for the deeper plan building, reflecting the reduction in external wall and window area relative to floor area. In addition, the range of impact of roofing specifications is large, with some of the C-rated roofing specifications

having amongst the highest impacts per metre squared of any element.

As a general principle, specifications with low-mass and minimal industrial processing achieve good environmental profiles. Pitched timber-framed roofs with clay, natural slate or concrete tiles produce the smallest environmental impacts because of the lightweight nature of the overall construction.

However, pitched timber-framed roofs may be impractical or visually problematic on some larger commercial or industrial projects. In these circumstances, lightweight steel systems provide the next best solution. These specifications would in fact perform better than they appear to in the tables were it not for the inclusion of timber-frame pitched roofs which perform so well.

Walls and roofs, as the primary building elements, are inextricably linked structurally and aesthetically and are the principal components of the weather-proofing building envelope. Hence, wall and roof systems must be compatible in both functional and visual terms and designers should take care not to compromise these essential requirements by mixing incompatible wall and roofing solutions purely on the grounds of perceived environmental preference.

## BREEAM

One credit is available in BREEAM for the use of A-rated specifications for over 80% (by area) of the roof. Appendix 4 provides further information on BREEAM assessment.

## Insulation

Specifiers should pay particular attention to the comments in the section on insulation in Appendix 1. However, the small mass of insulation needed to satisfy Building Regulation requirements means that compared with the mass of the materials used in the rest of the roof construction, the ratings are not sensitive to the type of insulation chosen, as long as the insulation is not ozone-depleting.

In such circumstances, the resulting increased climate change and ozone depletion impacts would affect the Summary Ratings by one increment, so that an 'A' Summary Rating would become a 'B', a 'B' would move to a 'C' and a 'C' would be so adversely affected as to move it into a 'sub-category'.

## Division of roofing specifications into subsections

Roofing specifications have been arranged into subsections for ease of use by designers. However, ratings have been arrived at through comparison of *all* roofing types shown across *all* subsections. The subsections are:

- Flat roofs — 'cold deck', 'inverted deck' and 'warm deck', the position of the insulation being the primary difference between the systems.
- 'Traditional' pitched roofs — e.g. roofs with a pitch of over 20°, including tiled roofs on a timber roof structure and profiled sheet roofing.
- Low pitched roofs — e.g. pitched profiled roof decking, composite cladding panels, etc.

# Flat roofs

| Element | Summary Rating | Climate Change | Fossil Fuel Depletion | Ozone Depletion | Human Toxicity to Air and Water | Waste Disposal | Water Extraction | Acid Deposition | Ecotoxicity | Eutrophication | Summer Smog | Minerals Extraction | Cost £/m² | Typical Replacement Interval | Recycled Input | Recyclability | Recycled Currently | Energy Saved by Recycling |
|---|---|---|---|---|---|---|---|---|---|---|---|---|---|---|---|---|---|---|
| **FLAT ROOF: COLD DECK** | | | | | | | | | | | | | | | | | | |
| Plasterboard, vapour control layer, insulation, plywood decking, timber joists, felt isolating layer, asphalt, chippings | A | A | A | A | A | A | A | A | C | B | B | A | 70-102 | 25 | C | C | C | A |
| Plasterboard, vapour control layer, insulation, plywood decking, timber joists, polyester reinforced bitumen felt, chippings | A | A | A | A | A | A | A | A | A | B | B | A | 73-92 | 15 | C | B | B | B |
| Plasterboard, vapour control layer, insulation, timber joists, plywood, single ply roofing membrane, chippings | A | A | A | A | A | A | A | A | A | B | B | A | 80-100 | 15 | C | A | B | A |
| **FLAT ROOF: INVERTED DECK** | | | | | | | | | | | | | | | | | | |
| Galvanised steel deck, asphalt, insulation, paving slabs | A | A | A | A | A | A | A | A | B | A | B | A | 100-152 | 30 | C | B | B | B |
| In situ reinforced concrete, asphalt, insulation, chippings | C | B | A | A | C | C | A | B | C | C | A | C | 89-139 | 30 | C | A | B | B |
| Permanent steel shuttering, in situ concrete, asphalt, insulation, paving slabs | C | B | A | A | C | C | A | B | B | C | B | C | 125-170 | 30 | C | A | B | B |
| Plasterboard, timber joists, plywood, asphalt, insulation, chippings | A | A | A | A | A | A | A | A | C | A | A | A | 73-92 | 30 | C | B | B | B |
| Plasterboard, timber joists, plywood, asphalt, insulation, paving slabs | A | A | A | A | A | A | A | A | C | A | A | A | 110-152 | 30 | C | B | C | B |
| Precast concrete hollow slab, asphalt, insulation, paving slabs | C | B | A | A | C | C | A | B | B | C | A | C | 125-185 | 30 | C | A | B | B |
| **FLAT ROOF: WARM DECK** | | | | | | | | | | | | | | | | | | |
| Galvanised steel deck, vapour barrier, insulation, felt isolating layer, asphalt, chippings | B | A | A | A | A | A | A | A | C | A | B | A | 77-102 | 25 | C | C | C | B |
| Galvanised steel deck, vapour barrier, insulation, felt isolating layer, polyester reinforced bitumen felt, chippings | B | B | B | A | A | A | A | B | A | A | B | A | 75-100 | 15 | C | A | B | C |
| In situ reinforced concrete deck, vapour barrier, insulation, felt isolating layer, polyester reinforced bitumen felt, chippings | C | B | B | A | B | B | A | B | A | B | A | B | 85-135 | 15 | C | A | A | C |
| In situ reinforced concrete slab, vapour barrier, insulation, asphalt, chippings | C | B | B | A | C | C | A | B | C | C | A | C | 95-125 | 25 | C | A | B | B |

*Continued*

| Element | Summary Rating | Climate Change | Fossil Fuel Depletion | Ozone Depletion | Human Toxicity to Air and Water | Waste Disposal | Water Extraction | Acid Deposition | Ecotoxicity | Eutrophication | Summer Smog | Minerals Extraction | Cost £/m² | Typical Replacement Interval | Recycled Input | Recyclability | Recycled Currently | Energy Saved by Recycling |
|---|---|---|---|---|---|---|---|---|---|---|---|---|---|---|---|---|---|---|
| In situ reinforced concrete, vapour barrier, insulation, single ply roofing membrane, chippings | C | B | B | A | C | C | A | B | A | C | A | C | 90–120 | 15 | C | A | A | C |
| Permanent steel shuttering, in situ concrete, vapour barrier, insulation, felt isolating layer, asphalt, chippings | C | B | B | A | C | C | A | B | C | C | B | C | 90–110 | 25 | C | A | B | B |
| Permanent steel shuttering, in situ concrete, vapour barrier, insulation, felt isolating layer, polyester reinforced bitumen felt, chippings | C | B | B | A | B | B | A | B | A | B | B | C | 85–105 | 15 | C | A | A | C |
| Plasterboard, timber joists, plywood decking, vapour control layer, insulation, felt isolating layer, asphalt, chippings | A | A | A | A | A | A | A | A | C | A | A | A | 73–92 | 25 | C | C | C | B |
| Plasterboard, timber joists, plywood decking, vapour control layer, insulation, felt isolating layer, polyester reinforced bitumen felt, chippings | B | B | B | A | A | A | A | B | A | A | A | A | 70–90 | 15 | C | B | B | C |
| Precast hollow concrete slab, vapour barrier, insulation, felt isolating layer, polyester reinforced bitumen felt, chippings | C | C | B | A | B | C | A | B | A | C | A | C | 85–120 | 15 | C | A | A | C |
| Precast hollow concrete slab, vapour barrier, insulation, felt isolating layer, asphalt, chippings | C | B | B | A | C | C | A | B | C | C | A | C | 88–123 | 25 | C | A | B | B |

The type of roof structure has a major effect on the impact of flat roof specifications. The best performing are the timber flat roofs. Steel deck alternatives perform intermediately. The poorest performers are the concrete flat roofs due to the high mass of material required. Concrete is a very low embodied energy material, but needs to be used in high mass in roofing and floor structures. Users should refer to the 'Upper floor' section of this edition for further information on selecting a concrete flat roof structure with low impacts.

The choice of the roofing membrane (the roof-covering material which is keeping out the weather, e.g. roofing felt, asphalt, etc.) is also relevant. When roofing membranes are replaced or repaired, the insulation, decking materials, flashings, etc. may also need replacement either due to deterioration caused by leaks or damage or simply because it is impractical to replace the membrane without replacement of other components within the roof construction. The lifespan of the roofing membrane is therefore of great importance to the environmental profile of flat roofs. Increased resource consumption in constructing a roof that will last longer will be offset by the reduction in materials used later in repairs and refurbishment. In terms of the impacts of the roofing membranes, asphalt generally has higher impacts than the lightweight reinforced bitumen felt. It should be noted that roofing felt will typically require less frequent replacement if stone chippings or paving slabs are used and the membrane is not exposed to the elements.

# 'Traditional' pitched roofs

| Element | Summary Rating | Climate Change | Fossil Fuel Depletion | Ozone Depletion | Human Toxicity to Air and Water | Waste Disposal | Water Extraction | Acid Deposition | Ecotoxicity | Eutrophication | Summer Smog | Minerals Extraction | Cost £/m² | Typical Replacement Interval | Recycled Input | Recyclability | Recycled Currently | Energy Saved by Recycling |
|---|---|---|---|---|---|---|---|---|---|---|---|---|---|---|---|---|---|---|
| Clay tiles, battens, sarking felt on timber roof structure with insulation between rafters | A | A | A | A | A | A | A | A | A | A | A | A | 60-90 | 60 | C | A | C | A |
| Concrete tiles, battens, sarking felt, on timber roof structure with insulation between rafters | A | A | A | A | A | A | A | A | A | A | A | A | 37-62 | 60 | C | A | C | B |
| Double skin profiled roof, coated aluminium inner and outer skin, insulation on steel roof structure | A | A | A | A | A | A | A | A | A | A | A | A | 60-75 | 40 | A | B | B | A |
| Double skin profiled roof, coated aluminium outer skin, steel inner skin, insulation on steel roof structure | A | A | A | A | A | A | A | A | A | A | B | A | 60-75 | 40 | A | B | A | A |
| Double skin profiled roof, coated steel, insulation on steel roof structure | A | A | A | A | A | A | A | A | A | A | C | A | 45-70 | 25 | B | B | A | A |
| Double skin profiled roof, mill finish aluminium outer skin, galvanised steel inner lining, insulation on steel roof structure | A | A | A | C | A | A | B | A | A | A | A | A | 60-85 | 40 | B | A | A | A |
| Double skin profiled roof, mill finish stainless steel outer skin, galvanised steel inner lining, insulation on steel roof structure | A | A | A | C | A | A | B | A | A | A | A | A | 90-112 | 40 | A | A | A | B |
| Double skin profiled roof, mill finish aluminium profiled outer skin, coated steel liner, insulation on steel roof structure | A | A | A | A | A | A | A | A | A | A | B | A | 55-80 | 40 | A | B | A | A |
| Fibre cement slates, battens, sarking felt on timber roof structure with insulation between rafters | B | A | B | A | A | A | A | B | B | B | A | A | 47-75 | 30 | C | A | C | C |
| Polymer/resin bonded slates, battens, sarking felt on timber roof structure with insulation between rafters | C | C | C | A | C | A | A | C | C | C | B | A | 52-81 | 35 | C | C | C | C |
| Slates, battens, sarking felt on timber roof structure with insulation within rafters | A | A | A | A | A | C | A | A | A | A | A | C | 70-100 | 60 | C | A | A | B |

Traditional roofing materials such as clay and concrete tiles and slate score well. Modern replacement materials such as polymer resin bonded slates score less well due to their greater use of energy- and resource-intensive materials.

Trussed rafter construction uses about 30% less timber than traditional 'cut' rafters, thus reducing the environmental impact of the roof structure. However, the contribution of the structure to the environmental impact of pitched roofs is relatively small, so ratings shown are applicable to either type of timber roof structure.

## Reclaimed and recycled materials

Reclaimed clay and concrete tiles may be more brittle than new materials, leading to shorter replacement intervals, but reclaimed tiles and slates will have lower environmental impacts than new.

## Low pitched roofs

| Element | Summary Rating | Climate Change | Fossil Fuel Depletion | Ozone Depletion | Human Toxicity to Air and Water | Waste Disposal | Water Extraction | Acid Deposition | Ecotoxicity | Eutrophication | Summer Smog | Minerals Extraction | Cost £/m² | Typical Replacement Interval | Recycled Input | Recyclability | Recycled Currently | Energy Saved by Recycling |
|---|---|---|---|---|---|---|---|---|---|---|---|---|---|---|---|---|---|---|
| Double skin profiled roof, coated aluminium inner and outer skin, insulation, breather membrane, on steel roof structure | A | A | A | A | A | A | A | A | A | A | A | A | 60-75 | 40 | A | B | B | B |
| Double skin profiled roof, coated aluminium profiled outer skin, steel inner skin, insulation, breather membrane, on steel roof structure | A | A | A | A | A | A | A | A | A | A | B | A | 60-75 | 40 | A | B | A | A |
| Double skin profiled roof, coated steel inner and outer skin, insulation, breather membrane, on steel roof structure | A | A | A | A | A | A | A | A | A | C | A | | 45-70 | 25 | B | B | A | A |
| Double skin profiled roof, mill finish aluminium profiled outer skin, steel inner skin, insulation, breather membrane, on steel roof structure | A | A | A | A | A | A | A | A | A | B | A | | 60-85 | 40 | A | B | A | A |
| Double skin profiled roof, mill finish stainless steel profiled outer skin, steel inner skin, insulation, breather membrane, on steel roof structure | A | A | A | A | A | A | A | A | A | B | A | | 90-125 | 40 | A | B | A | A |
| Coated steel composite roofing system, insulation, on steel roof structure | A | A | A | C | A | A | C | A | A | B | A | | 45-55 | 25 | C | A | A | B |
| Coated aluminium composite roof cladding, insulation, on steel roof structure | A | A | A | C | A | A | B | A | A | A | A | | 40-50 | 40 | A | B | A | A |
| Coated aluminium outer and steel liner composite roofing system, insulation, on steel roof structure | A | A | A | C | A | A | B | A | A | A | A | | 40-50 | 40 | B | A | A | A |

All metal deck and composite panels in this section perform well, scoring 'A' ratings, due principally to their low mass/lightweight construction. It would be expected that this type of roof construction would perform equally well with a timber roof structure.

# Medium- and low-mass elements

# Floor finishes and coverings

Functional unit: 1 m² of floor finish or covering including underlay, including any repair, refurbishment or replacement over a 60-year building life.

Importance of floor finishes (wool/nylon mix carpet with sponge-foam backing; 5-year typical replacement interval) within a typical building

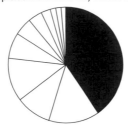

**Ecopoints per m² of Element**

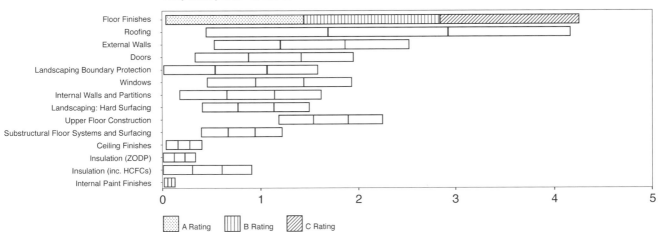

Summary Rating A B C ranges for different elements.

## Significant environmental issues for this element

Climate change, fossil fuel depletion and acidification.

Designers and specifiers of commercial developments often have no control over the specification of floor finishes which is normally undertaken as part of the fit-out contract. Therefore floor finishes have not been included within the pie charts normally provided for each building element.

The pie chart above shows embodied impact for elements of a typical building including floor finishes. The specification assumed is a wool/nylon mix carpet on a sponge-foam backing with a 5-year typical replacement interval. The pie chart shows that in this case, the floor finishes can contribute more than a third of the building's overall embodied impact over 60 years. Accordingly, although they

are a low-mass element, floor finishes can contribute significantly and should be given serious consideration. This is reinforced by the range of Summary Rating values for floor finishes — the largest of any element, with floor finish specifications having both the highest and some of the lowest Ecopoints/m² assessed.

Floor finishes have been indicated as a major source of VOC emissions which can have an effect on indoor air quality. Users should pay attention to the section on 'Indoor Air Quality Issues' in Appendix 1.

The choice of floor finish is generally determined by the intended use of the building and the practical requirements of an individual space. Designers and specifiers first establish whether a room requires a 'hard' or 'soft' floor finish, depending on, for example, whether the material needs to be waterproof or easily cleaned or whether particular visual, acoustic or comfort-related qualities are priorities. Having made this decision, the final choice of specification is made from within these basic groups. To reflect this process and to make the task of the specifier more straightforward, floor finishes and coverings have been grouped into the following product types:

- Hard floor finishes, including timber, sheet and tile materials and timber finishes
- Soft floor finishes, including carpets and mattings

The data have been analysed across the entire range of flooring products so it is possible to compare the environmental profiles of, say, a type of carpet with a particular tiled floor finish.

Many floor finishes are normally fitted or laid with underlays or backings to provide good wear and an even surface and these have been taken into account where appropriate.

# Hard floor finishes

| Element | Summary Rating | Climate Change | Fossil Fuel Depletion | Ozone Depletion | Human Toxicity to Air and Water | Waste Disposal | Water Extraction | Acid Deposition | Ecotoxicity | Eutrophication | Summer Smog | Minerals Extraction | Cost £/m² | Typical Replacement Interval | Recycled Input | Recyclability | Recycled Currently | Energy Saved by Recycling |
|---|---|---|---|---|---|---|---|---|---|---|---|---|---|---|---|---|---|---|
| Ceramic floor tiles | A | A | A | A | A | A | A | A | A | A | A | C | 22-78 | 20 | C | C | C | A |
| Hardboard sheathing 3.2 mm, linoleum 2.5 mm | A | A | A | C | B | A | A | A | A | B | A | A | 19-22 | 15 | B | C | C | B |
| Hardboard sheathing 3.2 mm, PVC sheet 2 mm | B | B | B | B | C | A | A | B | C | C | A | A | 17-19 | 10 | B | C | C | C |
| Hardboard sheathing 3.2 mm, synthetic rubber tiles | C | C | C | A | A | C | A | C | A | C | A | A | 28-37 | 10 | B | C | C | C |
| Hardboard sheathing 3.2 mm, cork tiles 6.4 mm | A | A | A | A | A | A | A | A | A | C | A | A | 26-30 | 10 | B | C | C | C |
| Hardboard sheathing 3.2 mm, plus PVC tiles, 2.5 mm | B | B | B | B | C | A | A | B | C | C | A | A | 18-21 | 10 | B | C | C | C |
| Hardwood (parquet) 25 mm | A | A | A | A | A | A | C | A | A | A | A | A | 48-75 | 20 | C | A | B | A |
| Hardwood (strip) 8 mm | A | A | A | A | A | A | A | A | A | A | A | A | 23-27 | 20 | C | A | B | A |
| Marble tiles | A | A | A | A | A | A | A | C | A | A | A | B | 235-301 | 30 | C | A | A | A |
| Quarry tiles | A | A | A | A | A | A | A | A | A | A | A | B | 23-41 | 30 | C | C | C | A |
| Softwood block flooring, 25 mm deep | A | A | A | A | A | A | B | A | A | A | A | A | 39-47 | 20 | C | A | B | A |
| Terrazzo tiles | A | A | A | A | A | B | A | A | A | A | A | C | 69-81 | 15 | C | B | C | B |

Of the 'hard' floor finishes, those derived from natural materials requiring minimum processing appear to perform very well, especially linoleum and cork. These finishes perform well even where the floor may be uneven and needs to be sheathed with hardboard before applying the surface materials.

Compared to all the other floor finishes, timber performs as one of the best options in all its forms; parquet, strip and block. Designers should be sure to specify timber from responsibly managed sources; this is particularly important when specifying hardwoods. Softwood block is one of the best performers overall.

A number of hard tile floor finishing materials perform well over the life cycle because of their durability — marble, terrazzo, ceramic and quarry tiles.

Polyvinyl chloride (PVC) sheet performs intermediately overall. PVC has been the subject of intense and controversial debate for several years. Readers should refer to recent publications from the DETR, the Environment Agency and Forum for the Future for specific information on the material and its use in construction.

# Soft floor coverings

| Element | Summary Rating | Climate Change | Fossil Fuel Depletion | Ozone Depletion | Human Toxicity to Air and Water | Waste Disposal | Water Extraction | Acid Deposition | Ecotoxicity | Eutrophication | Summer Smog | Minerals Extraction | Cost £/m² | Typical Replacement Interval | Recycled Input | Recyclability | Recycled Currently | Energy Saved by Recycling |
|---|---|---|---|---|---|---|---|---|---|---|---|---|---|---|---|---|---|---|
| 80/20 wool/nylon carpet, natural fibre underlay | A | A | B | A | A | B | A | A | A | A | A | A | 31–48 | 5 | C | C | C | C |
| 80/20 wool/nylon carpet, recycled rubber crumb underlay | A | A | B | A | A | B | A | A | A | A | A | A | 31–48 | 5 | A | B | C | C |
| 80/20 wool/nylon carpet, sponge foam underlay | C | C | C | A | A | C | A | C | A | A | A | A | 31–48 | 5 | C | B | C | B |
| Nylon carpet, natural fibre | A | A | B | A | A | A | A | A | A | A | A | A | 13–19 | 5 | B | C | C | C |
| Nylon carpet, recycled rubber crumb underlay | A | A | B | A | A | B | A | A | A | A | A | A | 13–19 | 5 | A | B | C | C |
| Nylon carpet, sponge foam underlay | C | C | C | A | A | C | A | C | A | A | A | A | 13–19 | 5 | C | B | C | B |
| Seagrass, hardboard sheathing | A | A | A | A | A | A | A | A | A | C | A | A | 35–40 | 5 | C | C | C | C |
| Sisal/jute, hardboard sheathing | A | A | A | A | A | A | A | A | A | C | A | A | 31–38 | 5 | C | C | C | B |
| Wool carpet, natural fibre | A | A | A | A | A | B | A | A | A | A | A | A | 26–34 | 5 | C | C | C | B |
| Wool carpet, recycled rubber crumb underlay | A | A | A | A | A | B | A | A | A | A | A | A | 26–34 | 5 | A | B | C | C |
| Wool carpet, sponge foam underlay | C | C | C | A | A | C | A | C | A | A | A | A | 26–34 | 5 | C | B | C | B |

Of these soft finishes, sisal/jute, seagrass and wool carpet produce the best results. Once again this is due to them being basically natural materials requiring the minimum of industrial processing.

The poorest performers are carpets with sponge/foam underlays/backings. The use of the term 'sponge foam' is something of a misnomer as the material is in fact an aerated plastic. Carpets can perform well, provided they are used with natural fibre or recycled rubber underlays. A wool carpet on natural fibre or recycled rubber crumb underlay is the best carpeting option overall.

## Substructural floor systems/floor surfacing

Functional unit: 1 m$^2$ of substructural floor system or floor surfacing, to provide a level surface for the laying of floor covering and, when appropriate, access to a void beneath the floor surface for servicing of the building. To include any repair, refurbishment or replacement over a 60-year building life

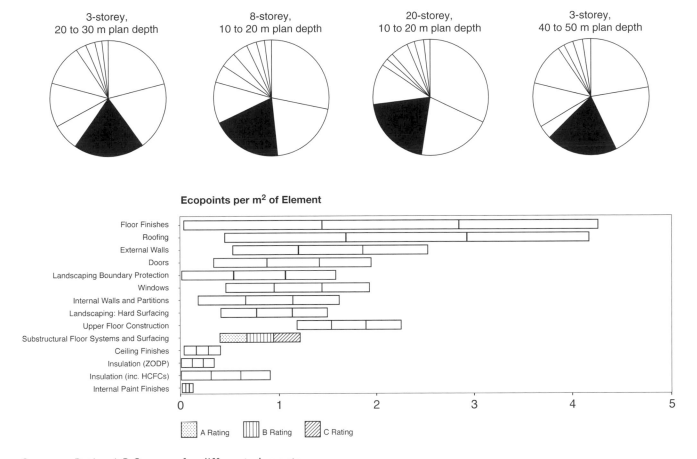

Summary Rating A B C ranges for different elements.

### Significant environmental impacts for this element

Climate change, acidification and fossil fuel depletion.

For each of the building types evaluated above, the use of a shallow raised access floor (chipboard and steel sheet on pedestals) contributed around 20% of the building's embodied impact. Designers should weigh up the embodied impacts of raised floors against considerations of convenience, adaptability and the capacity for individual control offered by these systems when compared with services provision located in ceilings or on walls. More flexible/adaptable solutions can offer environmental and financial benefits in that future changes can be accommodated at lower cost, involving less construction work and fewer new materials.

# Substructural floor systems/floor surfacing

| Element | Summary Rating | Climate Change | Fossil Fuel Depletion | Ozone Depletion | Human Toxicity to Air and Water | Waste Disposal | Water Extraction | Acid Deposition | Ecotoxicity | Eutrophication | Summer Smog | Minerals Extraction | Cost £/m² | Typical Replacement Interval | Recycled Input | Recyclability | Recycled Currently | Energy Saved by Recycling |
|---|---|---|---|---|---|---|---|---|---|---|---|---|---|---|---|---|---|---|
| Chipboard on timber battens | A | B | B | A | A | A | A | B | A | A | A | A | 20-24 | 30 | A | C | C | A |
| Deep (500 mm) raised access floor with steel stringers | C | C | C | B | C | C | C | C | B | C | C | C | 38-69 | 30 | A | A | A | C |
| Deep (500 mm) raised access floor without stringers | C | C | C | C | C | C | C | C | C | C | B | B | 38-69 | 30 | A | B | B | B |
| Plywood on timber battens | A | A | A | C | A | A | A | A | B | B | A | A | 33-41 | 30 | C | C | B | A |
| Shallow (150 mm) raised access floor with steel stringers | C | C | C | B | C | C | C | C | B | C | C | C | 33-64 | 30 | A | A | A | C |
| Shallow (150 mm) raised access floor without steel stringers | C | C | C | C | B | B | C | C | C | C | B | B | 33-64 | 30 | A | B | C | B |
| Shallow raised flooring system – chipboard on galvanised steel profiled decking | B | B | B | A | A | B | C | B | A | A | B | B | 30-35 | 30 | A | B | B | B |
| Shallow raised flooring system – plywood on galvanised steel profiled decking | A | A | A | C | B | A | C | A | B | C | B | B | 35-40 | 30 | C | A | A | C |

The range of options included here is small, but the significant contribution of this element made their inclusion worthwhile. This section also provides designers with some guidance on the relative embodied impacts of raised 'computer floors' commonly used to provide access for power and IT connections and HVAC systems.

The ratings show the best-performing specifications to be timber systems with the chipboard/galvanised steel decking performing intermediately. All the raised access floors perform less well. This is due to the intensive use of materials and manufacturing processes involved.

# Windows and curtain walling

Functional unit: $1\,m^2$ of double-glazed window or clear-glazed curtain walling, to satisfy Building Regulations and to include any repair, refurbishment or replacement over a 60-year building life.

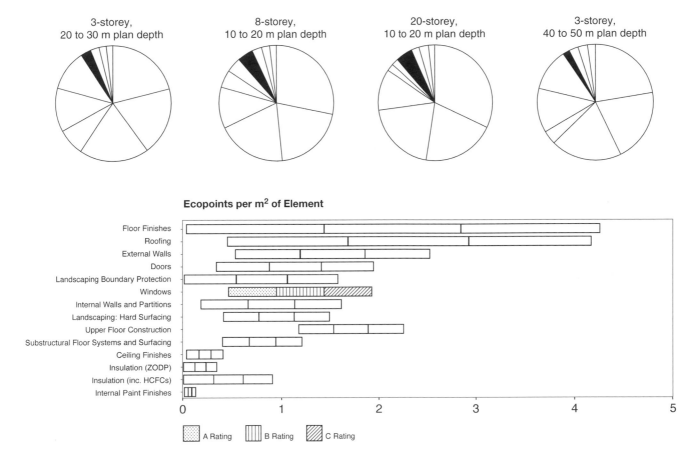

Summary Rating A B C ranges for different elements.

## Significant environmental issues for this element

Climate change, acidification, fossil fuel depletion and human toxicity.

The pie charts are based on buildings with a glazing ratio of 30%. For such buildings, windows are one of the elements with a less important role in the overall embodied impact of buildings. However, the narrower the plan depth, as with external walls, the greater the impact, as the surface area of the building increases relative to the floor area.

Although at a glazing ratio of 30%, windows may not seem to represent a significant proportion of the building impact, it is possible for a high percentage of the façade to consist of glazed areas, particularly in commercial developments with glazed curtain walling. In such cases, the choice of window specification can make a significant contribution to the reduction of the building's overall embodied impact.

The specifications overleaf can be applied equally to opening or fixed windows or to glazed curtain walling.

# Windows and glazed curtain walling

| Element | Summary Rating | Climate Change | Fossil Fuel Depletion | Ozone Depletion | Human Toxicity to Air and Water | Waste Disposal | Water Extraction | Acid Deposition | Ecotoxicity | Eutrophication | Summer Smog | Minerals Extraction | Cost £/m² | Typical Replacement Interval | Recycled Input | Recyclability | Recycled Currently | Energy Saved by Recycling |
|---|---|---|---|---|---|---|---|---|---|---|---|---|---|---|---|---|---|---|
| Aluminium framed window/curtain walling | B | C | B | A | C | A | A | C | A | A | A | A | 235–300 | 35 | A | A | A | A |
| Aluminium composite window/curtain walling with timber internal frame, painted inside | B | B | B | A | B | A | A | B | A | A | A | A | 290–350 | 35 | B | A | B | B |
| Glass block window | C | B | C | A | C | C | A | B | C | C | A | C | 185–420 | 25 | C | B | C | A |
| Hardwood timber framed window/curtain walling | A | A | A | A | A | A | A | A | A | A | A | A | 300–370 | 30 | C | A | B | B |
| Painted preserved softwood timber framed window/curtain walling | A | A | A | A | A | A | A | A | A | B | C | A | 185–245 | 25 | C | A | B | C |
| PVC-U framed window | C | C | C | C | C | A | A | C | C | A | A | A | 480–550 | 25 | B | C | C | B |
| Steel framed window/curtain walling | B | B | B | A | A | A | C | A | A | C | B | A | 200–250 | 30 | C | A | A | B |
| Structural glazing (silicone jointed) | B | B | B | A | B | B | A | B | B | B | A | B | 330–560 | 25 | C | A | C | C |

In our appraisal of this small but representative sample, timber windows are found to be the lowest embodied impact option due to timber being a natural product requiring relatively low energy levels in manufacture.

The steel and aluminium windows perform intermediately in achieving their 'B' ratings while PVC-U scores a 'C'. Although primary aluminium production is intensive, in particular in terms of embodied energy, aluminium extrusions within the UK construction industry contain approximately 30% post-consumer recycled material, thus reducing the levels of energy required.

The glazing within a typical double-glazed window accounts for less than 20% of the embodied impact of the window. The type of glazing therefore does little to affect the Summary Rating of specifications, although the choice of single, double or triple glazing will obviously have a significant effect on the thermal performance of the window. The use of coatings on glazing to enhance thermal characteristics, etc. is also unlikely to make any difference to the overall environmental performance of the window.

Whilst glass production has not been dealt with as a separate section, designers should note that the environmental profile of glass would show a clear advantage over the use of polycarbonates, which require high levels of energy in manufacture and record poor emission levels.

Users may note the differences in window Summary Ratings between this edition and *The Green Guide to Housing Specification*. This can be explained due to differences in the expected replacement intervals and between typical specifications for the commercial and domestic market.

# Internal walls and partitioning

Functional unit: 1 m² of internal wall or partitioning, to satisfy Building Regulations, and to include any repair, refurbishment or replacement over a 60-year building life.

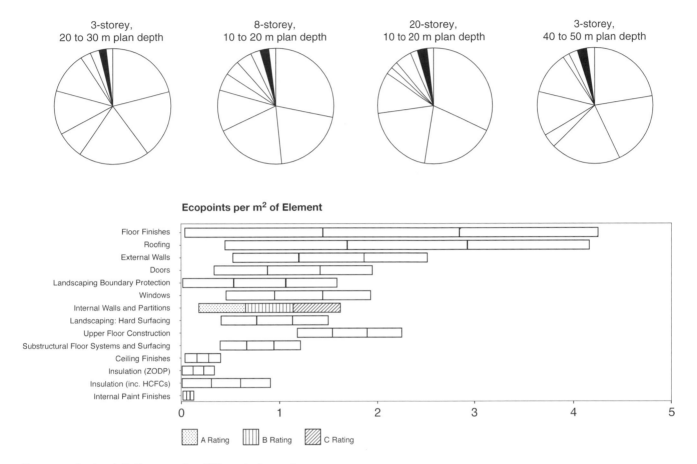

Summary Rating A B C ranges for different elements.

## Significant environmental issues for this element

Climate change, minerals extraction and waste disposal.

The majority of office developments are now open plan and this reduced use of internal walls and partitions within the typical building is reflected in the significance of internal wall specifications in the pie charts above. For an office designed with a cellular floor plan, the importance of the internal walls within the overall building embodied impact would be substantially increased.

The functional unit has been left intentionally undefined. Internal walls and partitioning may be transparent, trans-

lucent or opaque, may achieve particular fire resistance or compartmentation standards or may provide particular acoustic qualities and hence not necessarily be substitutable.

A wide range of internal partitioning systems have been compared in this section, and so specifications have been arranged according to whether they were loadbearing, non-loadbearing or demountable and proprietary types of partition, simply to enable specifiers to locate the required specification more easily. All ratings were derived through comparison with the entire range of internal wall and partitioning systems shown.

# Loadbearing partitions

| Element | Summary Rating | Climate Change | Fossil Fuel Depletion | Ozone Depletion | Human Toxicity to Air and Water | Waste Disposal | Water Extraction | Acid Deposition | Ecotoxicity | Eutrophication | Summer Smog | Minerals Extraction | Cost £/m² | Typical Replacement Interval | Recycled Input | Recyclability | Recycled Currently | Energy Saved by Recycling |
|---|---|---|---|---|---|---|---|---|---|---|---|---|---|---|---|---|---|---|
| Aerated blockwork partition, plasterboard on dabs, paint | A | A | A | A | A | A | A | A | A | A | A | A | 41-53 | 60 | B | B | B | B |
| Brickwork, plaster, paint | B | A | A | A | A | B | A | A | A | A | A | A | 45-60 | 60 | C | A | A | A |
| Dense blockwork, plasterboard on dabs, paint | A | A | A | A | A | B | A | A | A | A | A | A | 47-56 | 60 | C | A | A | B |
| Fairfaced brickwork | A | A | A | A | A | B | A | A | A | A | A | A | 26-36 | 60 | C | A | A | A |
| Fairfaced reinforced concrete | C | A | A | A | B | C | B | A | A | A | A | C | 80-95 | 60 | C | A | A | A |
| Lightweight blockwork partition, plasterboard on dabs, paint | B | B | A | A | A | B | A | A | A | A | A | A | 41-53 | 60 | A | A | A | B |

In previous studies, fairfaced brickwork and dense and aerated blockwork partitions have been outperformed by the lower-mass alternatives such as timber stud. New data (which show the improvements in manufacture) have produced results for brickwork and blockwork specifications which enable them to achieve comparable impacts.

Reinforced concrete performs most poorly amongst the loadbearing partitions. Although concrete is a relatively low embodied energy material, the additional mass of the material proved the decisive difference in this comparison. Moreover, construction and site factors may make the use of reinforced concrete for internal partitions impractical.

Of the blockwork and brickwork options, the dense and aerated blockwork and the fairfaced brickwork specifications are found to be generally comparable, with only the lightweight blockwork being marginally outperformed. Aerated blocks are significantly lighter and use less material than dense or lightweight blocks, giving a better environmental performance than other blockwork, even though the manufacturing is more intensive. Aerated blockwork may, of course, be structurally unsuitable for some loadbearing situations, in which case dense blockwork or fairfaced brickwork would be the preferred options. Lightweight blocks use low-density aggregates such as pumice. The extraction, manufacture and transport impacts for these raw materials are generally higher than for the raw materials used in dense blocks. Dense blocks tend to use more locally sourced aggregates and this has influenced the difference in scores between the two options.

Timber stud partitions used in a loadbearing capacity would probably be the best environmental option due to low mass and use of low-impact materials. However, timber stud may have limitations in terms of structural performance and is most commonly used in residential or other low-load situations.

# Non-loadbearing partitions

| Element | Summary Rating | Climate Change | Fossil Fuel Depletion | Ozone Depletion | Human Toxicity to Air and Water | Waste Disposal | Water Extraction | Acid Deposition | Ecotoxicity | Eutrophication | Summer Smog | Minerals Extraction | Cost £/m² | Typical Replacement Interval | Recycled Input | Recyclability | Recycled Currently | Energy Saved by Recycling |
|---|---|---|---|---|---|---|---|---|---|---|---|---|---|---|---|---|---|---|
| Enamelled steel partition, chipboard core | C | C | C | A | A | A | C | C | A | B | C | A | 365-600 | 15 | B | A | B | A |
| Enamelled steel partition, plywood core | B | B | B | A | A | A | C | A | A | B | C | A | 375-610 | 15 | C | A | A | A |
| 'Frameless' glazed partitioning system, silicon jointed, aluminium base channel | A | A | A | A | B | A | A | A | B | A | A | A | 245-290 | 30 | C | A | C | C |
| Glass blockwork wall | C | B | C | B | C | B | A | B | C | C | A | B | 155-203 | 30 | C | A | C | A |
| Hardwood veneered MDF framed glazed partitioning, double glazed | C | B | B | A | C | B | A | B | C | C | A | B | 282-313 | 15 | C | A | C | C |
| Softwood framed, double glazed partition, safety glass | B | B | B | A | B | A | A | B | B | B | A | A | 250-310 | 20 | C | A | C | C |
| Softwood framed, single glazed partition, safety glass | A | A | A | A | A | A | A | A | A | A | A | A | 150-210 | 20 | C | A | C | C |
| Steel jumbo stud partition, plasterboard and skim, glass wool insulation, paint | A | A | A | A | A | A | A | A | A | A | B | A | 74-100 | 30 | C | C | C | C |
| Steel jumbo stud, 2 sheets plasterboard each face, glass wool insulation (90 minutes' fire protection), paint | A | A | A | A | A | A | A | A | A | A | A | A | 83-109 | 60 | C | C | C | C |
| Steel stud, plasterboard and skim, glass wool insulation, paint | A | A | A | A | A | A | A | A | A | A | B | A | 40-70 | 15 | C | C | C | C |
| Steel stud, plasterboard, taped joints, glass wool insulation, paint | A | A | A | A | A | A | A | A | A | A | B | A | 40-70 | 15 | C | C | C | C |
| Timber stud, plasterboard and skim, glasswool insulation, paint | A | A | A | A | A | A | A | A | A | A | A | A | 35-65 | 15 | C | C | C | C |
| Timber stud, plywood, glasswool insulation | A | A | A | A | A | A | A | A | A | A | A | A | 42-48 | 15 | C | B | B | B |

Lowest-impact specifications in this section include both timber and steel stud partitions. Among the worst performers, the glass blockwork scores poorly due to the thickness and high mass of the material and the very high levels of energy required in the manufacturing processes. Similarly, the poor performance of the chipboard-cored enamelled steel panels is explained by the high levels of energy required in the manufacturing process and by the mass of the chipboard core and enamelled steel facings (two skins). However, the robust, low-maintenance quality of this form of construction offers the advantage of longevity — important in 'tougher' environments such as public thoroughfares, underground stations, etc.

# Proprietary and demountable partitions

| Element | Summary Rating | Climate Change | Fossil Fuel Depletion | Ozone Depletion | Human Toxicity to Air and Water | Waste Disposal | Water Extraction | Acid Deposition | Ecotoxicity | Eutrophication | Summer Smog | Minerals Extraction | Cost £/m² | Typical Replacement Interval | Recycled Input | Recyclability | Recycled Currently | Energy Saved by Recycling |
|---|---|---|---|---|---|---|---|---|---|---|---|---|---|---|---|---|---|---|
| Aluminium proprietary glazed partitioning system, double glazed, safety glass | C | C | C | B | C | A | A | C | B | C | A | A | 150-190 | 20 | C | A | C | B |
| Aluminium proprietary glazed partitioning system, single glazed, safety glass | B | B | B | B | C | A | A | B | A | B | A | A | 90-125 | 20 | C | A | C | B |
| Chipboard panel, steel frame | B | C | B | A | A | A | A | B | A | A | A | A | 30-36 | 15 | A | A | C | A |
| Chipboard panel, timber frame | B | C | B | A | A | A | A | B | A | A | A | A | 24-30 | 15 | A | A | C | A |
| Proprietary glazed partitioning system, steel framed, single glazed, safety glass | B | A | A | B | A | A | B | A | A | A | B | A | 180-240 | 20 | C | A | B | C |
| Proprietary partitioning system, aluminium framed, plasterboard panels with cardboard honeycomb core, paint | B | B | B | A | B | A | A | B | A | A | A | A | 43-105 | 20 | C | C | C | A |
| Vinyl finish chipboard panels with flaxboard core, aluminium framing | C | C | C | C | A | A | A | C | A | A | A | A | 40-100 | 15 | A | A | C | A |

The performance of these types of partition falls within the intermediate to poor categories. Demountable partitions can be seen to have advantages and disadvantages. Over the life of a building, demountable partitioning may be more flexible in use and may need a lower rate of renewal because it can be reused in a new location. Alternatively, it may be perceived as temporary and hence replaced at greater frequency. These considerations have, however, not been taken into account in this assessment and a typical replacement rate has been used.

# Suspended ceilings and ceiling finishes

Functional unit: 1 m² of suspended ceiling or ceiling finish, to satisfy Building Regulations, and to include any repair, refurbishment or replacement over a 60-year building life.

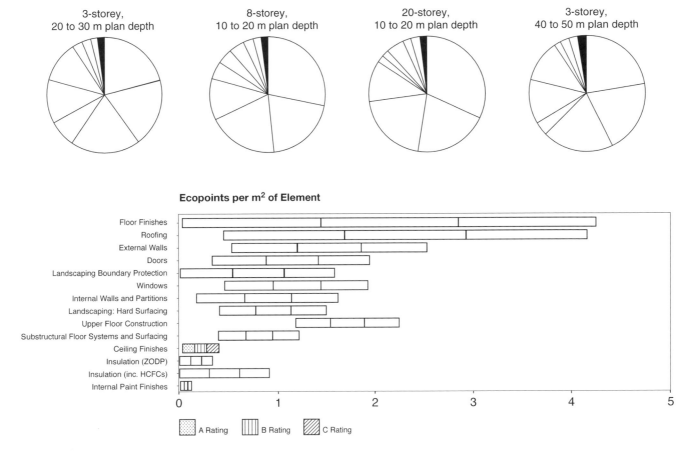

Summary Rating A B C ranges for different elements.

## Significant environmental issues for this element

Climate change.

The pie charts above show that the ceilings of commercial buildings are one of the elements with the smallest embodied impact, reflecting the relatively low mass, and the range of Summary Rating values is also one of the smallest.

A range of ceiling finishes and suspended ceilings have been assessed together in this section. Suspended ceiling systems are specified widely, particularly in commercial property. The range of available systems is very extensive — only the main alternatives are presented here.

# Suspended ceilings

| Element | Summary Rating | Climate Change | Fossil Fuel Depletion | Ozone Depletion | Human Toxicity to Air and Water | Waste Disposal | Water Extraction | Acid Deposition | Ecotoxicity | Eutrophication | Summer Smog | Minerals Extraction | Cost £/m² | Typical Replacement Interval | Recycled Input | Recyclability | Recycled Currently | Energy Saved by Recycling |
|---|---|---|---|---|---|---|---|---|---|---|---|---|---|---|---|---|---|---|
| Direct finish: 16 mm fibrous plaster to soffit | A | A | A | A | A | A | A | A | A | A | A | A | 125-150 | 40 | C | C | C | C |
| Direct finish: plasterboard on timber battens | A | A | A | A | A | A | A | A | A | A | A | A | 21-24 | 40 | C | C | C | C |
| Jointless suspended ceiling: lightweight plaster on expanded metal lath | B | A | B | A | A | C | A | A | A | A | A | C | 23-36 | 25 | C | B | B | B |
| Jointless suspended ceiling: plaster on expanded metal lath | B | A | B | A | A | C | A | A | A | A | A | C | 23-36 | 25 | C | B | B | B |
| Jointless suspended ceiling: plasterboard | A | A | A | A | A | A | A | A | A | A | A | B | 23-36 | 25 | C | C | C | B |
| Suspended ceiling, concealed grid: aluminium tile | B | B | B | A | C | A | A | C | A | B | A | A | 50-60 | 25 | A | A | A | A |
| Suspended ceiling, concealed grid: gypsum based tile | A | A | A | A | A | A | A | A | A | A | A | B | 56-67 | 25 | C | C | C | B |
| Suspended ceiling, concealed grid: mineral wool based tile | B | A | B | A | B | C | A | B | A | C | B | A | 24-38 | 25 | B | C | C | C |
| Suspended ceiling, concealed grid: steel tile | B | A | C | A | A | A | C | A | A | B | C | A | 36-47 | 25 | C | A | A | A |
| Suspended ceiling, concealed grid: woodwool tile | C | C | A | C | B | B | A | B | C | C | A | A | 24-38 | 25 | C | C | C | A |
| Suspended ceiling, exposed grid: gypsum based tile | A | A | A | A | A | A | A | A | A | A | A | B | 56-67 | 25 | C | C | C | B |
| Suspended ceiling, exposed grid: mineral wool tile | B | A | B | A | B | C | A | B | A | C | B | A | 19-30 | 25 | B | C | C | C |
| Suspended ceiling, exposed grid: vinyl faced gypsum based tile | A | A | B | C | A | A | A | A | A | A | A | B | 19-30 | 25 | C | C | C | C |
| Suspended ceiling, exposed grid: woodwool based tile | C | C | A | C | B | B | A | B | C | C | A | A | 19-30 | 25 | C | C | C | A |
| Suspended ceiling, linear system: aluminium strip | B | B | C | A | C | A | A | C | A | B | A | A | 36-47 | 25 | A | A | A | A |
| Suspended ceiling, linear system: steel strip | B | B | C | A | B | B | C | B | A | B | C | B | 36-47 | 25 | C | A | A | A |
| Suspended ceiling, louvred system: aluminium louvre | B | A | B | A | C | A | A | C | A | B | A | A | 55-66 | 25 | A | A | A | A |
| Suspended ceiling, open cell: aluminium tile | B | B | C | A | C | A | A | C | A | B | A | A | 39-84 | 25 | A | A | A | A |
| Suspended ceiling, open cell: MDF tile | B | B | B | A | A | A | A | B | A | A | A | A | 72-91 | 25 | B | A | C | A |
| Suspended ceiling, open cell: mineral wool based tile | B | A | B | A | B | C | A | B | A | C | B | A | 39-84 | 25 | B | C | C | C |

The best-performing specifications overall are the plasterboard and gypsum-based systems and the simple plastered soffit. The additional materials required for the lath-based plaster systems means they perform less well. The other suspended systems perform less well, with the worst ratings attributed to the woodwool systems, one of the heaviest products.

Suspended systems offer advantages over the traditional plastered soffit, being an economic and easy to install method of concealment of building services or of lowering ceilings for visual reasons. Suspended ceilings also offer the advantages of adaptability and can be easily removed. In the case of the jointless suspended plasterboard ceiling, access to the ceiling void above will require a hatch or removable panel, unlike many of the other systems where access is afforded simply by lifting out a ceiling tile.

# Doors

Functional unit: 1 m² of door, to satisfy Building Regulations, and to include any repair, refurbishment or replacement over the 60-year building life.

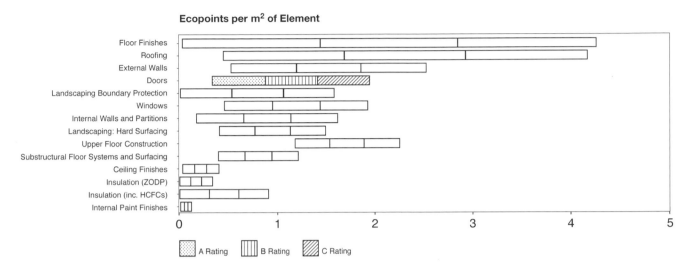

**Ecopoints per m² of Element**

Summary Rating A B C ranges for different elements.

## Significant environmental issues for this element

Climate change, acidification and fossil fuel depletion.

Within the typical office development, the use of open-plan layouts has reduced the number of doors, and their impact on the overall building embodied impact is therefore very small. However, the Summary Ratings range graph shows there is a significant difference between an A- and C-rated door specification. Significant environmental issues for doors relate to the use of fossil fuels for energy and feedstock.

For a cellular office with doors to every individual room, the importance of door specification, along with internal wall specification, will be substantially increased.

# Doors

| Element | Summary Rating | Climate Change | Fossil Fuel Depletion | Ozone Depletion | Human Toxicity to Air and Water | Waste Disposal | Water Extraction | Acid Deposition | Ecotoxicity | Eutrophication | Summer Smog | Minerals Extraction | Cost £/m² | Typical Replacement Interval | Recycled Input | Recyclability | Recycled Currently | Energy Saved by Recycling |
|---|---|---|---|---|---|---|---|---|---|---|---|---|---|---|---|---|---|---|
| **FIRE DOORS – 1 HOUR** | | | | | | | | | | | | | | | | | | |
| Flush, chipboard faced, chipboard core | C | C | C | A | C | C | A | C | C | C | B | A | 235-260 | 20 | A | A | C | A |
| Flush, chipboard faced, flaxboard core | B | B | A | C | A | C | C | C | A | A | C | A | 235-260 | 20 | C | C | C | A |
| Flush, chipboard faced, softwood core | A | A | A | A | A | A | A | A | A | A | A | A | 235-260 | 20 | C | A | A | A |
| Flush, MDF faced, chipboard core | C | C | C | A | C | C | A | C | C | C | C | A | 250-275 | 20 | A | A | C | A |
| Flush, MDF faced, flaxboard core | B | B | A | C | A | C | C | C | A | A | C | A | 250-275 | 20 | C | C | C | A |
| Flush, MDF faced, softwood core | A | A | A | A | A | A | A | A | A | A | B | A | 250-275 | 20 | C | A | A | A |
| Flush, plywood faced, chipboard core | C | C | C | A | C | C | A | C | C | C | B | A | 270-295 | 20 | A | A | C | A |
| Flush, plywood faced, flaxboard core | B | B | A | C | A | C | C | C | A | B | B | A | 270-295 | 20 | C | C | C | A |
| Flush, plywood faced, softwood core | A | A | A | A | B | A | A | A | A | B | A | A | 270-295 | 20 | C | A | A | A |
| **FIRE DOORS – 0.5 HOUR** | | | | | | | | | | | | | | | | | | |
| Flush, chipboard faced, chipboard core | C | C | C | A | C | B | A | C | C | C | B | A | 48-77 | 20 | A | A | C | A |
| Flush, chipboard faced, softwood core | A | A | A | A | A | A | A | A | A | A | A | A | 200-225 | 20 | B | A | A | A |
| Flush, MDF faced, chipboard core | C | C | C | A | B | B | A | C | C | B | C | A | 53-82 | 20 | A | A | C | A |
| Flush, MDF faced, flaxboard core | A | A | A | B | A | A | B | B | A | A | C | A | 53-82 | 20 | C | C | C | A |
| Flush, MDF faced, softwood core | A | A | A | A | A | A | A | A | A | A | B | A | 215-240 | 20 | C | A | A | A |
| Flush, plywood faced, chipboard core | C | C | C | A | C | B | A | C | C | C | A | A | 59-88 | 20 | A | A | C | A |
| Flush, plywood faced, flaxboard core | A | A | A | B | A | A | B | B | A | A | A | A | 59-88 | 20 | C | C | C | A |
| Flush, plywood faced, softwood core | A | A | A | A | A | A | A | A | A | A | A | A | 225-250 | 20 | C | A | A | A |
| **GLAZED DOORS** | | | | | | | | | | | | | | | | | | |
| Hardwood frame, fully glazed with wired glass | A | A | A | A | B | B | A | A | B | A | A | C | 500-625 | 20 | C | A | B | C |
| Softwood frame, fully glazed with wired glass | A | A | A | A | B | B | A | A | B | A | A | C | 400 | 20 | C | A | B | C |
| **STANDARD INTERNAL DOORS** | | | | | | | | | | | | | | | | | | |
| Standard flush, chipboard faced, chipboard core | C | C | C | A | B | B | A | C | B | B | A | A | 31-40 | 20 | A | A | C | A |
| Standard flush, chipboard faced, flaxboard core | A | A | A | B | A | A | B | B | A | A | A | A | 31-40 | 20 | B | C | C | A |
| Standard flush, MDF faced, chipboard core | B | C | B | A | B | B | A | C | B | B | B | A | 33-42 | 20 | A | A | C | A |

*Continued*

| Element | Summary Rating | Climate Change | Fossil Fuel Depletion | Ozone Depletion | Human Toxicity to Air and Water | Waste Disposal | Water Extraction | Acid Deposition | Ecotoxicity | Eutrophication | Summer Smog | Minerals Extraction | Cost £/m² | Typical Replacement Interval | Recycled Input | Recyclability | Recycled Currently | Energy Saved by Recycling |
|---|---|---|---|---|---|---|---|---|---|---|---|---|---|---|---|---|---|---|
| Standard flush, MDF faced, flaxboard core | A | A | A | B | A | A | B | B | A | A | B | A | 33-42 | 20 | C | C | C | A |
| Standard flush, plywood faced, chipboard core | B | B | B | A | C | B | A | B | C | C | A | A | 38-47 | 20 | A | A | C | A |
| Standard flush, plywood faced, flaxboard core | A | A | A | B | A | A | B | A | A | A | A | A | 38-47 | 20 | C | C | C | A |

The best-performing specifications overall include the fully glazed timber-framed doors, due primarily to timber being a low-impact product and the relatively low impact of the glazing. Other specifications achieving an 'A' rating include all those utilising a softwood core — irrespective of the facing material. The core, therefore, is a primary determinate of embodied impact, the mass of the core being some 3 to 4 times that of the door-facing.

Softwood is the lowest-impact core material. Flaxboard is the second best core option and chipboard provides the poorest performing alternative.

Of the facing materials, plywood and chipboard appear to marginally outperform MDF which performs slightly worse against the *summer smog* parameter, due to higher VOC emissions and a higher solvent and resin content.

Further information on responsible timber specification is provided in Appendix 1, and is particularly relevant to these specifications.

# Other materials and elements

# Internal paint finishes

Functional unit: the painting of 1 m² of surface with white paint to an opacity of 98%, and to include any repair, refurbishment or replacement over the 60-year building life.

**Ecopoints per m² of Element**

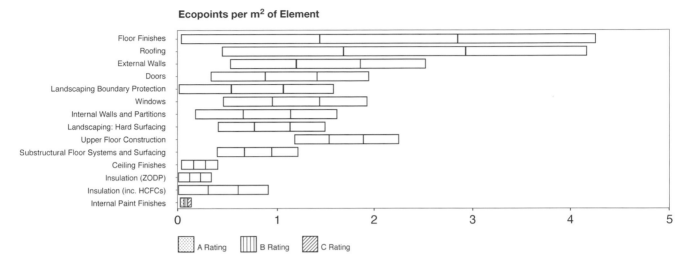

Summary Rating A B C ranges for different elements.

## Significant environmental Issues for this element

Summer smog, climate change and fossil fuel depletion.

It has proved difficult to obtain systematic data for the wide range of paints used in buildings today. The data used for this study were adapted from the EC Ecolabelling study (Ecobilan, 1993). This study gathered data systematically across most of the Environmental Profiles issues for a limited range of internal paints finishes. Where no data have been gathered, for example relating to toxicity, the issue ratings have been left blank.

Compared to the other elements, the range of Summary Ratings for paints spans a much smaller range of values. Summer smog, arising from the VOC emissions during paint application, is the impact that has the greatest effect on the result.

Many manufacturers now produce paints that are free of chemicals such as ammonia, formaldehyde and phenols — which, at high levels of exposure, can be irritants and can cause breathing difficulties. Designers should ensure that the paints specified are well suited to their application and used in accordance with manufacturers' instructions. Designers should also exercise care when writing specifications for paint removers and adhesives as many of the substances used may contain flammable or toxic solvents.

Careful consideration should also be given to the disposal of unused paint, brush-cleaning solvents, adhesives, etc. during building operations. Practices such as cans of unused paint being thrown into site waste containers for landfill or combustion or being poured into the public drainage system, cause pollution or toxic emissions and can be specifically prohibited. Designers should consider including clauses relating to this important issue within the written contract specification.

# Internal paint finishes

| Element | Summary Rating | Climate Change | Fossil Fuel Depletion | Ozone Depletion | Human Toxicity to Air and Water | Waste Disposal | Water Extraction | Acid Deposition | Ecotoxicity | Eutrophication | Summer Smog | Minerals Extraction | Cost £/m² | Typical Replacement Interval | Recycled Input | Recyclability | Recycled Currently | Energy Saved by Recycling |
|---|---|---|---|---|---|---|---|---|---|---|---|---|---|---|---|---|---|---|
| Gloss solvent-borne paint alkyd resin, isoparaffinic | B | B | B | | | B | B | B | | C | B | B | | 5 | | | | |
| Gloss solvent-borne paint alkyd resin, white spirit < 1% | B | B | B | | | B | B | B | | C | B | B | | 5 | | | | |
| Gloss water-borne paint styrene-acrylic resin | A | A | A | | | A | A | A | | A | A | A | | 5 | | | | |
| High solid paint, high solid resin, white spirit < 1% | A | A | A | | | A | A | A | | A | A | A | | 5 | | | | |
| Matt linseed oil emulsion | A | A | A | | | A | A | A | | A | A | C | | 5 | | | | |
| Matt solvent-borne paint, limed oil, isoparaffinic | C | C | C | | | C | C | C | | A | C | C | | 5 | | | | |
| Matt solvent-borne paint plioway resin, isoparaffinic | C | C | C | | | A | A | C | | B | C | A | | 5 | | | | |
| Matt water-borne paint microvoid resin | A | A | A | | | A | A | B | | A | A | A | | 5 | | | | |
| Matt water-borne paint, styrene-acrylic resin | A | A | A | | | A | A | B | | B | A | A | | 5 | | | | |
| Semi-gloss solvent-borne paint, alkyd resin, white spirit < 5% | B | B | B | | | A | A | B | | B | B | A | | 5 | | | | |

Despite the small sample size, a number of key findings did emerge from this study, which tend to support the current consensus regarding the environmental impacts of paints. As a general principle, paints that utilise water or vegetable oil as a base and are produced using simple processes achieve the best environmental profiles. Those that involve the use of high-energy, complex chemical processes tend to perform least well environmentally.

Top-scoring paints include linseed (vegetable) oil-based emulsion paint. Water-borne paints showed smaller impacts than solvent-borne paints, with the VOC emissions resulting from the solvent causing high impacts.

# Insulation

Functional unit: 1 m$^2$ of insulation with sufficient thickness to provide a thermal resistance value of 1.48 m$^2$K/W, equivalent to approximately 50 mm of insulation with a conductivity ($\kappa$ value) of 0.034 W/mK.

**Ecopoints per m$^2$ of Element**

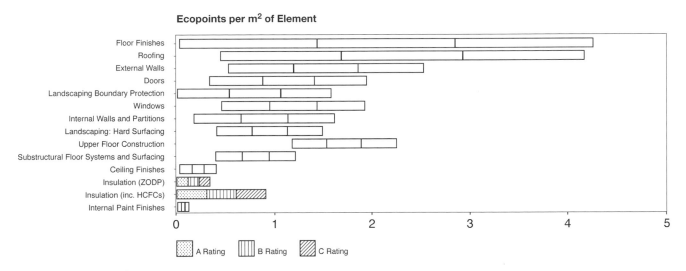

Summary Rating A B C ranges for different elements.

## Significant environmental issues for this element

Ozone depletion (for insulation including HCFCs), climate change and fossil fuel depletion (for ZODP insulation).

Insulation is generally very low-density material and only small masses are needed to provide high levels of insulation. For this reason, the contribution of the insulation to the impact of elements is generally small. The use of insulation in the building fabric will significantly reduce the environmental impact from the operation of the building over its lifetime. This benefit will outweigh the embodied environmental impact for all the insulation materials included in this guide.

Within the *Green Guide*, an 'average' insulation material has been used in the specifications. This average insulation had zero ozone-depletion potential (ZODP). However, a number of insulation materials are not ZODP and have very significant environmental impacts. The attributes of alternative forms of insulation have therefore been sepa-

rated out and considered as a separate category in this section. The graph of Summary Rating ranges shows how significant the inclusion within insulation materials of HCFCs, which cause ozone depletion, can be to their environmental impact.

The basis of comparison is a common thermal resistance so that all the insulations included can be compared on an equal footing, as they would all transmit the same amount of heat if they were used in the same construction. The insulation materials have different conductivities, so they are able to provide the same thermal resistance with different thicknesses of material.

## BREEAM

One credit is available in BREEAM if the specification of insulation avoids the use of ozone-depleting substances. Appendix 4 provides further information on BREEAM assessment.

# All insulations (including those using HCFCs)

| Element | Summary Rating | Climate Change | Fossil Fuel Depletion | Ozone Depletion | Human Toxicity to Air and Water | Waste Disposal | Water Extraction | Acid Deposition | Ecotoxicity | Eutrophication | Summer Smog | Minerals Extraction | Cost £/m² | Typical Replacement Interval | Recycled Input | Recyclability | Recycled Currently | Energy Saved by Recycling |
|---|---|---|---|---|---|---|---|---|---|---|---|---|---|---|---|---|---|---|
| Any foamed insulation (HCFC blown) | C | C | B | C | C | A | A | B | C | C | A | A | 9-10 | 60 | C | C | C | C |
| Cavity blown glass wool insulation, assumed density 25 kg/m³ | A | A | A | A | A | A | A | A | A | A | A | A | 5-6 | 60 | C | C | C | C |
| Cavity blown rock wool insulation, assumed density 40 kg/m³ | A | A | A | A | A | A | A | A | A | A | A | A | 5-6 | 60 | B | C | C | C |
| Cellular glass insulation, density 105 kg/m³ | A | A | A | A | A | A | A | A | A | A | A | C | 17-20 | 60 | C | A | A | A |
| Cellular glass insulation, density 120 kg/m³ | A | A | B | A | A | A | A | B | A | A | A | C | 17-20 | 60 | C | A | A | A |
| Corkboard insulation with density 120 kg/m³ | A | A | A | A | A | A | A | A | A | A | A | A | 15-17 | 60 | C | A | C | C |
| Expanded polystyrene (EPS), density 15 kg/m³ | A | A | A | A | A | A | A | A | A | A | A | A | 4-9 | 60 | C | C | C | C |
| Expanded polystyrene (EPS), density 20 kg/m³ | A | A | A | A | A | A | A | A | A | A | A | A | 4-9 | 60 | C | C | C | C |
| Extruded polystyrene (XPS) (ZODP) with density less than 40 kg/m³ | B | C | C | A | A | A | A | C | A | A | A | A | 21-33 | 60 | C | C | C | C |
| Glass wool insulation, density 12 kg/m³ | A | A | A | A | A | A | A | A | A | A | A | A | 4-5 | 60 | C | C | C | C |
| Glass wool insulation, density 25 kg/m³ | A | A | A | A | A | A | A | A | A | A | A | A | 4-5 | 60 | C | C | C | C |
| Glass wool insulation, density 32 kg/m³ | A | A | A | A | A | A | A | A | A | A | A | A | 4-5 | 60 | C | C | C | C |
| Glass wool insulation, density 48 kg/m³ | A | A | A | A | A | A | A | A | A | A | A | A | 4-5 | 60 | C | C | C | C |
| Glass wool insulation, density 80 kg/m³ | A | A | A | A | A | A | A | A | A | A | A | A | 4-5 | 60 | C | C | C | C |
| Glass wool insulation, density 145 kg/m³ | A | A | A | A | B | B | A | A | A | B | A | A | 5-6 | 60 | C | C | C | C |
| Glass wool insulation, density 160 kg/m³ | A | A | A | A | B | B | A | A | A | B | A | A | 5-6 | 60 | C | C | C | C |
| Pentane blown (ZODP) polyurethane (PU) insulation | A | A | A | A | B | A | C | A | A | A | A | A | 9-10 | 60 | C | C | C | C |
| Recycled cellulose insulation | A | A | A | A | A | A | A | A | A | A | A | A | 6-8 | 60 | A | C | C | C |
| Rock wool insulation, density 33 kg/m³ | A | A | A | A | A | A | A | A | A | A | A | A | 4-5 | 60 | B | C | C | C |
| Rock wool insulation, density 45 kg/m³ | A | A | A | A | A | A | A | A | A | A | A | A | 4-5 | 60 | B | C | C | C |
| Rock wool insulation, density 60 kg/m³ | A | A | A | A | A | A | A | A | A | A | A | A | 4-5 | 60 | B | C | C | C |
| Rock wool insulation, density 80 kg/m³ | A | A | A | A | A | B | A | A | A | A | B | A | 5-6 | 60 | B | C | C | C |
| Rock wool insulation, density 100 kg/m³ | A | A | A | A | B | B | A | A | A | A | B | B | 5-6 | 60 | B | C | C | C |
| Rock wool insulation, density 130 kg/m³ | A | A | A | A | B | B | A | A | A | B | B | B | 5-6 | 60 | B | C | C | C |

*Continued*

| Element | Summary Rating | Climate Change | Fossil Fuel Depletion | Ozone Depletion | Human Toxicity to Air and Water | Waste Disposal | Water Extraction | Acid Deposition | Ecotoxicity | Eutrophication | Summer Smog | Minerals Extraction | Cost £/m² | Typical Replacement Interval | Recycled Input | Recyclability | Recycled Currently | Energy Saved by Recycling |
|---|---|---|---|---|---|---|---|---|---|---|---|---|---|---|---|---|---|---|
| Rock wool insulation, density 140 kg/m³ | A | A | A | A | B | C | A | A | A | B | C | B | 6-7 | 60 | B | C | C | C |
| Rock wool insulation, density 160 kg/m³ | A | A | A | A | B | C | A | A | A | B | C | B | 6-7 | 60 | B | C | C | C |
| Rock wool insulation, density 180 kg/m³ | A | A | A | A | C | C | A | A | A | B | C | C | 7-8 | 60 | B | C | C | C |
| Rock wool insulation, density 200 kg/m³ | A | A | A | A | C | C | A | A | A | B | C | C | 7-8 | 60 | B | C | C | C |

In a comparison of all common insulation materials, HCFC blown insulation foams are the poorest performers. HCFCs are most commonly used in closed cell foams like polyurethane (PU) and extruded polystyrene (XPS) as they help to decrease the conductivity of the foam, meaning a smaller thickness of insulation can be used to provide the same level of insulation. Their high impact is due to the ozone depletion and climate change caused by the release of HCFCs into the atmosphere. Appendix 1 provides more information on the issues associated with the use of HCFCs, but specifiers should be aware of the impact of these types of blowing agents, and are recommended to specify insulation materials with ZODP.

In order to offer meaningful guidance on the choice of ZODP insulation, overleaf the same insulation specifications have been compared without the inclusion of HCFC blown foams.

# Zero ozone depletion potential (ZODP) insulations

| Element | Summary Rating | Climate Change | Fossil Fuel Depletion | Ozone Depletion | Human Toxicity to Air and Water | Waste Disposal | Water Extraction | Acid Deposition | Ecotoxicity | Eutrophication | Summer Smog | Minerals Extraction | Cost £/m² | Typical Replacement Interval | Recycled Input | Recyclability | Recycled Currently | Energy Saved by Recycling |
|---|---|---|---|---|---|---|---|---|---|---|---|---|---|---|---|---|---|---|
| Cavity blown rock wool insulation, assumed density 40 kg/m³ | A | A | A | A | A | A | A | A | A | A | A | A | 5-6 | 60 | B | C | C | C |
| Cellular glass insulation, density 105 kg/m³ | B | A | A | A | A | A | A | A | A | A | A | C | 17-20 | 60 | C | A | A | A |
| Cellular glass insulation, density 120 kg/m³ | B | B | B | A | A | A | A | B | A | A | A | C | 17-20 | 60 | C | A | A | A |
| Corkboard insulation with density 120 kg/m³ | A | B | A | A | A | A | A | A | B | A | A | A | 15-17 | 60 | C | A | C | C |
| Expanded polystyrene (EPS) density 15 kg/m³ | A | A | A | A | A | A | A | A | A | A | A | A | 4-9 | 60 | C | C | C | C |
| Expanded polystyrene (EPS) density 20 kg/m³ | A | A | A | A | A | A | A | A | A | A | A | A | 4-9 | 60 | C | C | C | C |
| Extruded polystyrene (XPS) (ZODP) with density less than 40 kg/m³ | C | C | C | A | A | A | A | C | A | A | A | A | 21-33 | 60 | C | C | C | C |
| Glass wool insulation, density 12 kg/m³ | A | A | A | A | A | A | A | A | A | A | A | A | 4-5 | 60 | C | C | C | C |
| Glass wool insulation, density 25 kg/m³ | A | A | A | A | A | A | A | A | A | A | A | A | 4-5 | 60 | C | C | C | C |
| Glass wool insulation, density 32 kg/m³ | A | A | A | A | A | A | A | A | A | A | A | A | 4-5 | 60 | C | C | C | C |
| Glass wool insulation, density 48 kg/m³ | A | A | A | A | A | A | A | A | A | A | A | A | 4-5 | 60 | C | C | C | C |
| Glass wool insulation, density 80 kg/m³ | A | A | A | A | A | A | A | A | A | A | A | A | 4-5 | 60 | C | C | C | C |
| Glass wool insulation, density 145 kg/m³ | A | A | A | A | B | B | A | A | A | C | A | A | 5-6 | 60 | C | C | C | C |
| Glass wool insulation, density 160 kg/m³ | B | A | A | A | B | B | A | A | A | C | A | A | 5-6 | 60 | C | C | C | C |
| Pentane blown (ZODP) polyurethane (PU) insulation | A | A | A | C | C | A | C | A | C | B | A | A | 9-10 | 60 | C | C | C | C |
| Recycled cellulose insulation | A | A | A | A | A | A | A | A | A | A | A | A | 6-8 | 60 | A | C | C | C |
| Rock wool insulation, density 33 kg/m³ | A | A | A | A | A | A | A | A | A | A | A | A | 4-5 | 60 | B | C | C | C |
| Rock wool insulation, density 45 kg/m³ | A | A | A | A | A | A | A | A | A | A | A | A | 4-5 | 60 | B | C | C | C |
| Rock wool insulation, density 60 kg/m³ | A | A | A | A | A | A | A | A | A | A | A | A | 4-5 | 60 | B | C | C | C |
| Rock wool insulation, density 80 kg/m³ | A | A | A | A | B | B | A | A | A | B | B | A | 5-6 | 60 | B | C | C | C |
| Rock wool insulation, density 100 kg/m³ | A | A | A | A | B | B | A | A | A | B | B | B | 5-6 | 60 | B | C | C | C |
| Rock wool insulation, density 130 kg/m³ | A | A | A | A | B | B | A | A | A | B | B | B | 5-6 | 60 | B | C | C | C |
| Rock wool insulation, density 140 kg/m³ | A | A | A | A | C | C | A | A | A | C | C | B | 6-7 | 60 | B | C | C | C |
| Rock wool insulation, density 160 kg/m³ | B | A | A | A | C | C | A | A | A | C | C | B | 6-7 | 60 | B | C | C | C |
| Rock wool insulation, density 180 kg/m³ | B | A | A | A | C | C | A | A | A | C | C | C | 7-8 | 60 | B | C | C | C |
| Rock wool insulation, density 200 kg/m³ | B | A | A | A | C | C | A | A | A | C | C | C | 7-8 | 60 | B | C | C | C |

The key variable in this category appears to be the density of the insulation in addition to the nature of the materials used. The best performers overall are the low-density variants of rock wool and glass wool. When used in flat roof construction, where the insulant may need some intrinsic strength, the higher-density variants of these materials must be used and these perform less well. Low-density expanded polystyrene (EPS) and ZODP polyurethane (PU) foam can be used where intrinsic strength is required, and both perform well.

Cellular glass and ZODP extruded polystyrene (XPS) provide the poorest performance against most of the chosen environmental criteria.

# Landscaping: hard surfacing

Functional unit: 1 m² of hard surfacing, suitable for the parking of cars, to satisfy Building Regulations, and to include any repair, refurbishment or replacement over the 60-year building life.

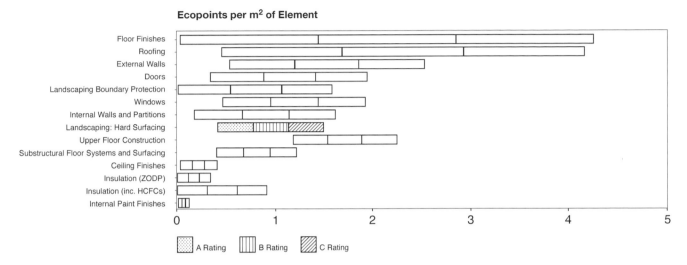

Summary Rating A B C ranges for different elements.

## Significant environmental issues for this element

Minerals extraction, climate change and waste disposal.

Ratios of 9 car parking spaces to every 10 occupants or 1 space per 25 m² of gross floor area are now common for office developments. These mean the area of hard surfacing can be around 80% of the floor area of the office. These large areas of hard surfacing can obviously have significant impacts. As would be expected for these specifications, minerals extraction and waste disposal are two of the most significant environmental issues for this element.

## Landscaping: hard surface

| Element | Summary Rating | Climate Change | Fossil Fuel Depletion | Ozone Depletion | Human Toxicity to Air and Water | Waste Disposal | Water Extraction | Acid Deposition | Ecotoxicity | Eutrophication | Summer Smog | Minerals Extraction | Cost £/m$^2$ | Typical Replacement Interval | Recycled Input | Recyclability | Recycled Currently | Energy Saved by Recycling |
|---|---|---|---|---|---|---|---|---|---|---|---|---|---|---|---|---|---|---|
| Asphalt | C | C | C | A | C | C | A | C | C | C | C | A | 45-50 | 20 | C | B | B | A |
| Brick pavers | B | B | B | A | A | B | A | A | A | A | C | A | 50-60 | 40 | C | A | A | A |
| Concrete pavers | A | A | A | A | A | B | A | A | A | A | B | A | 22-34 | 40 | A | A | A | A |
| Concrete paving slabs | A | A | A | A | A | A | A | A | A | A | A | A | 20-28 | 40 | C | A | A | A |
| Granite setts | B | A | A | A | A | B | A | A | A | A | A | B | 68-75 | 40 | C | A | A | A |
| Gravel | B | A | A | A | A | C | B | A | A | A | A | C | 8-11 | 10 | C | B | B | C |
| In-situ concrete | C | C | A | A | B | C | B | B | A | C | B | C | 28-33 | 60 | C | A | A | A |
| Proprietary grassed concrete paving | A | A | A | A | A | B | C | A | A | B | C | A | 70-100 | 30 | C | C | C | A |
| Stone paving slabs | A | A | A | C | A | A | A | A | A | A | A | A | 90-105 | 60 | C | A | A | A |

The best performers here are the concrete paving specifications (except where the concrete was in-situ and therefore of high mass) and the UK-produced Portland Stone paving slabs. Granite and brick perform intermediately, due primarily to the greater thickness of the material. Asphalt performs worst due to more intensive industrial processing and the need to replace the material more often.

A significant embodied impact can be attributed to the hardcore base used beneath landscaping materials. Impacts can be reduced if recycled aggregates are used. Whilst the use of recycled aggregate, both for hardcore and within concrete, will improve the environmental profile of the material, designers should be aware that quality control and performance factors will need to be taken into account in order to ensure adequate strength and stability of materials.

# Landscaping: boundary protection

Functional unit: these ratings can be applied to boundary protection up to 2 m in height and, where the specification is appropriate, to balustrading.

**Ecopoints per m² of Element**

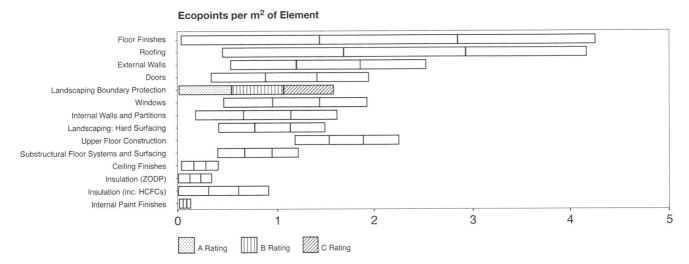

Summary Rating A B C ranges for different elements.

## Significant environmental issues for this element

Climate change, minerals extraction and waste disposal.

The perimeter of an 'out-of-town' site is often long enough for the area boundary protection to be significant compared to the area of external wall of the building it surrounds. Boundary protection can therefore make a significant contribution to the overall impacts of a typical out-of-town commercial development.

The graph shows that the range for this element is broad, with some specifications having very low Summary Rating values. As would be expected for many of these specifications using masonry, the important environmental issues relate to the mass of minerals extracted and the waste generated at the end of life of the specifications.

# Landscaping: boundary protection

| Element | Summary Rating | Climate Change | Fossil Fuel Depletion | Ozone Depletion | Human Toxicity to Air and Water | Waste Disposal | Water Extraction | Acid Deposition | Ecotoxicity | Eutrophication | Summer Smog | Minerals Extraction | Cost £/m² | Typical Replacement Interval | Recycled Input | Recyclability | Recycled Currently | Energy Saved by Recycling |
|---|---|---|---|---|---|---|---|---|---|---|---|---|---|---|---|---|---|---|
| Brickwork wall, 1 brick thick | C | C | C | A | C | C | C | C | A | C | A | B | 160-200 | 45 | C | A | B | A |
| Brickwork wall, 1/2 brick thick | B | B | B | A | B | B | B | B | A | B | A | A | 90-159 | 30 | C | A | B | A |
| Drystone walling | A | A | A | A | A | A | B | A | A | A | A | C | 111-230 | 60 | C | A | C | B |
| Galvanised steel post and wire strung at 1-ft intervals | A | A | A | A | A | A | A | A | A | A | A | A | 8-10 | 20 | C | A | A | B |
| Galvanised steel railings | B | B | B | B | C | A | A | C | C | B | A | A | 90-100 | 45 | C | A | A | B |
| Galvanised wire chainlink fence with steel posts | A | A | A | A | A | A | A | A | A | A | A | A | 10-12 | 30 | C | A | A | A |
| Hedging or any living barrier | A | A | A | A | A | A | A | A | A | A | A | A | 16-44 | 60 | A | A | C | A |
| Perforated concrete blockwork wall | A | B | A | A | A | A | A | A | A | A | A | A |  | 40 | A | C | C | A |
| Plastic coated chainlink fence with metal posts | A | A | A | A | A | A | A | A | A | A | A | A | 11-13 | 20 | C | C | A | C |
| Pre-treated timber close boarded fencing | A | A | A | C | A | A | A | A | A | A | C | A | 16-20 | 20 | C | B | C | A |
| Pre-treated timber palisade or picket fencing | A | A | A | A | A | A | A | A | A | A | A | A | 14-16 | 20 | C | B | C | A |
| Pre-treated timber post and panel fencing | A | A | A | A | A | A | A | A | A | A | A | A | 25-27 | 20 | C | B | C | A |
| Pre-treated timber post and rail fencing | A | A | A | A | A | A | A | A | A | A | A | A | 8-12 | 20 | C | B | C | A |
| Pre-treated timber post and trellis fencing | A | A | A | A | A | A | A | A | A | A | A | A | 24-26 | 12 | C | B | C | A |
| Stone and mortar wall | B | A | A | A | C | B | A | A | A | A | C | | 112-190 | 60 | C | A | C | A |

As with many elements, the performance of these specifications generally reflects the mass of material used. Stone walls, with low impacts from processing, still have the highest impacts in terms of mineral extraction. The waste generated at the end of life for the brickwork and stone and mortar walls is also high. The metal chainlink and wire fences still perform well because such low masses of metals are used. The railings, which need a relatively higher mass of metal, therefore have higher impacts.

All the timber used in these specifications has been pre-treated, ensuring good protection against decay. Untreated timber could be used, with slightly lower initial impacts, but it will have a shorter life and thus worse overall performance over a 60-year life.

Living barriers, such as hedging or willow, are one of the best performers, even taking account of a rigorous electrical trimming regime. In addition, they can provide a valuable habitat for wildlife.

# Part IV
# Appendices

## Appendix 1: General notes relating to the use of specific materials and particular environmental issues

The methodology behind *The Green Guide to Specification* does not assess individual materials, but evaluates the impacts of functionally equivalent specifications. There are, however, issues that are particularly relevant to specific materials, and the authors have therefore highlighted some of these below.

### Timber

Many of the environmental impacts of special significance to wood and to forestry practice are not covered by the environmental issues included within the *Green Guide* and the sustainable sourcing of timber should be considered alongside the profile results when evaluating individual sources of timber. The environmental profiles for specifications using timber in this edition of the *Green Guide* have been based on timber sourced from sustainably managed forests.

Where possible, designers should give preference to timber products obtained from well-managed, sustainable sources which are independently certified under schemes such as the Forest Stewardship Council (FSC), the Finnish National Certification Scheme or UK Woodland Assurance Scheme which enables FSC Certification.

Where independently certified timber is not available, designers should give preference to timber from suppliers who have adopted a formal Environmental Purchasing Policy, such as the Forests Forever Environmental Purchasing Policy.

For further information on the sourcing of sustainable timber, contact:

- Forests Forever: www.forestsforever.co.uk, Tel.: 020 7839 1891
- Forest Stewardship Council: www.fsc-uk.demon.co.uk, Tel.: 01686 413916
- BRE's Centre for Timber Technology and Construction: timber@bre.co.uk

The environmental profiles for timber also take account of typical transport based on current patterns of imports and home production. The transport impacts of locally sourced timber are therefore likely to be better than those shown within this guide.

The use of timber preservatives in situations where timber, left untreated, would be likely to decay greatly extends the life of the timber (with modest additional initial embodied impact), thereby reducing replacement intervals and the total impact over a 60-year life. Factory application of preservatives both ensures their efficacy and minimises any risk of environmental damage. The use of timber preservatives is strictly regulated under the Control of Pesticides Regulations.

### Indoor air quality issues

It has been known for some time that materials such as paints and furnishings can produce emissions, primarily formaldehyde and VOCs, which can affect indoor air quality. The Environmental Profiles Methodology, along with most LCA methodologies dealing with construction materials, is currently unable to take account of the indoor air quality issues associated with the use of materials within buildings due to the lack of an accepted method of assessment within an LCA context. However, this is an area of the methodology that BRE is keen to develop in the future.

For designers and specifiers who have an interest in this area, data are now available on emissions from some materials, which can be obtained from BRE's Centre for Safety, Health and Environment. Alternatively, specifiers and manufacturers can commission a comprehensive emissions measuring and testing service to ascertain emission levels so that they can select low-polluting products and materials.

For further information on indoor air quality issues and availability of measuring and testing and data on emissions levels from materials contact BRE's Centre for Safety, Health and Environment or visit www.bre.co.uk/env health/service5.html.

## Insulation: CFCs, HCFCs and HFCs

Chlorofluorocarbons (CFCs), hydrochlorofluorocarbons (HCFCs) and hydrofluorocarbons (HFCs) are chemicals that have been or are used in buildings — as refrigerants in air-conditioning systems and as blowing agents in insulation materials. In insulation materials, these gases are used because they reduce the conductivity of the closed cell foams in which they are used and therefore increase their thermal efficiency.

Originally, CFCs were used as blowing agents, but since 2000 in the UK they have been phased out under the Montreal Protocol because they are a major cause of ozone depletion. As a result, HCFCs have been used to replace them. However, as can be seen from the table below, HCFCs still cause ozone depletion and are also very strong greenhouse gases causing climate change. Because of this, the overall embodied impact of foams that use these gases is over three times greater than foams that use alternative blowing agents such as pentane or carbon dioxide.

As a result of the ozone depletion caused by HCFCs, they too are covered by the Montreal Protocol, and the EU has banned their sale from 2010. Manufacturers of foams are considering alternatives to HCFCs, and HFCs are possible replacements. Although they do not cause ozone depletion, as can be seen below, they are still significant greenhouse gases causing climate change.

| Relative ozone depletion and climate change impacts of the release of 1 kg various blowing agents | | |
|---|---|---|
| | Ozone depletion | Climate change |
| CFC-11 | 1 | 3,400 |
| HCFC-141b | 0.11 | 370 |
| HFC-143a | 0 | 300 |
| Pentane | 0 | 0 |
| Carbon dioxide | 0 | 1 |

Because these gases are used in closed rather than open cell foams, it is unlikely that significant amounts of these gases are released whilst these insulation foams are installed within buildings. However, significant amounts are released during manufacture of the gases, production of the foams, and at the end of life of the building when the foams are broken up and placed into landfill.

## PVC

PVC is used in a wide variety of applications from construction materials through to food packaging. PVC is stable during use and is fairly inert. Concerns have been expressed regarding possible environmental and health impacts related to the manufacture, use and disposal of PVC and the additives combined with PVC to form PVC products. Issues receiving attention include the production of toxic by-products during incineration and accidental fires and the use of additives (e.g. phthalate plasticisers and heavy metal stabilisers).

The PVC industry has responded vigorously to the debate surrounding its product and is actively demonstrating the on-going environmental improvements that are taking place across the industry. The issues surrounding PVC are currently undergoing review by the European Commission.

A particular problem with the debate surrounding PVC is that Life Cycle Assessment is often seen as a solution that will provide a definitive answer on the relative advantages and disadvantages of using PVC and alternative materials. In fact, the issues that caused the debate have often not been included within LCA (e.g. toxic releases, workforce exposure and fire hazards). This has been the case in a number of recent UK studies and reviews, including the DETR study referenced below. This study recommends that policy decisions regarding PVC consider a broad range of issues and consider not only technical information and its robustness but also public opinion and the reasons that such opinion is formed.

The results in the *Green Guide* do consider some toxic effects, but these should in no way be seen as comprehensive, for any of the material alternatives considered. Many of the chemicals used in society have not undergone a risk assessment and assessment techniques are still developing.

Some further information sources are:

British Plastics Federation, www.bpf.co.uk, Tel.: 020 7457 5000.

Entec UK Ltd. (2001) Life cycle assessment of polyvinyl chloride and alternatives: summary report. DETR, www.detr.gov.uk, Tel.: 0870 1226236.

Environment Agency (2001) Plastics in the environment. Environment Agency, www.environment-agency.gov.uk, Tel.: 01454 624400.

Greenpeace, www.greenpeace.org, Tel.: 020 7865 8100.

Natural Step (2000) PVC: an evaluation using the Natural Step framework. The Natural Step, Cheltenham, www.naturalstep.org.uk, Tel.: 01242 262744.

## Appendix 2: Worked example of the generation of a *Green Guide* rating for an internal wall specification

*Generation of the environmental profile for the specification*

The specification used to demonstrate the generation of a *Green Guide* rating is a painted, plasterboarded dense concrete blockwork wall, 100 mm thick.

The table below shows the amount of materials used in a metre squared of the wall and the expected replacement interval. Materials such as the paper to tape the joints and the plaster dabs to fix the plasterboard are too low in mass for the results to be sensitive to their inclusion.

| Installed mass and replacement intervals for painted, plasterboarded dense concrete blockwork wall, 100 mm thick | | |
|---|---|---|
| | Installed mass/m$^2$ (kg) | Replacement interval (years) |
| Dense block | 195 | 60 |
| Mortar | 12 | 60 |
| Plasterboard | 18.2 | 60 |
| Paint | 0.36 | 5 |

To account for the replacement of materials, the number of times each material would be installed over the life of the building is then calculated by dividing the building life by the expected life. So for this partition, with a building life of 60 years, we would expect it to be repainted 60/5 = 12 times over the life of the building.

To reflect the probability of replacement actually occurring, a factor of 0.5 is then added to this figure. For the paint, the number of applications would be 60/5 + 0.5 = 12.5. This indicates that there is a 50% chance that the cladding panel would be replaced 12 times over the life of the building, and a 50% chance that it would be replaced 13 times.

If the expected life of the component is more than 60 years, it is expected to last for the life of the building without replacement and the factor is not taken into account.

The mass per metre squared of each material used over the life of the building can now be calculated. The table below shows the calculation results for our example internal wall.

| Mass of materials used over 60-year life for a painted, plasterboarded dense concrete blockwork wall, 100 mm thick | | | |
|---|---|---|---|
| | Installed mass/m$^2$ (kg) | Replacement factor | 60-year life mass/m$^2$ (kg) |
| Dense block | 195 | 60/60 +0.5 = 1.5 | 195 × 1.5 = 292.5 |
| Mortar | 12 | 60/60 +0.5 = 1.5 | 12 × 1.5 = 18 |
| Plasterboard | 18.2 | 60/60 +0.5 = 1.5 | 18.2 × 1.5 = 27.3 |
| Paint | 0.36 | 60/5 +0.5 = 12.5 | 0.36 × 12.5 = 4.5 |

The table below shows extracts from environmental profiles, held by BRE, for materials used in the specification. Environmental impact issues are represented by the columns of the table.

| Environmental impacts of raw materials for a painted, plasterboarded dense concrete blockwork wall, 100 mm thick | | | |
|---|---|---|---|
| | Climate change (kg $CO_2$/tonne) | Waste disposal (kg/tonne) | Etc. |
| Dense block | 46 | 51 | . . . |
| Mortar | 170 | 69 | |
| Plasterboard | 150 | 95 | |
| Paint | 1200 | 850 | |

Using the data from the above table giving the environmental impacts for the production of a tonne of each material, the impacts from the production of materials over the life of the building can now be calculated (see table below).

| Selected production impacts over 60-year building life for a painted, plasterboarded dense concrete blockwork wall, 100 mm thick | | | |
|---|---|---|---|
| | 60-year life mass/m$^2$ (kg) | Climate change per tonne for material (kg $CO_2$/tonne) | Climate change/m$^2$ (kg $CO_2$/m$^2$) |
| Dense block | 292.5 | 46 | $0.2925 \times 46 = 13.5$ |
| Mortar | 18 | 170 | $0.018 \times 170 = 3.0$ |
| Plasterboard | 27.3 | 150 | $0.0273 \times 150 = 4.1$ |
| Paint | 4.5 | 1200 | $0.0045 \times 1200 = 5.4$ |
| | | Total | 26.0 |

The table above only refers to the impacts associated with the production of materials from the cradle (man's first intervention – for example quarrying) to the factory gate. It does not take account of the impacts associated with the transport of materials from the factory gate to the construction site, or the impacts associated with the disposal of materials after replacement or demolition at the end of life of the building.

Using a similar approach, in line with the BRE Environmental Profiles Methodology, these impacts are calculated for each material over the life of the building, giving a total picture of the embodied impacts associated with that particular specification.

The table below shows the total breakdown of the specification over the 60-year building life.

| Selected total impacts over 60-year building life for a painted, plasterboarded dense concrete blockwork wall, 100 mm thick | |
|---|---|
| | Climate change (kg $CO_2$/m$^2$) |
| 'Cradle to factory gate' | 26 |
| Transport to site | 3.0 |
| End of life disposal | 0 |
| Total | 29 |

## *Generation of the* Green Guide *rating for each environmental issue*

Once all the specifications within a particular element have been assessed separately, then the *Green Guide* ratings for each environmental issue can be calculated.

Within each element, in this case internal walls, covering the subsections 'Loadbearing partitions', 'Non-loadbearing partitions' and 'Demountable partitions', all the results are compared for each environmental issue. For each issue, the lowest and highest impact are found. For example, for internal walls, looking at climate change, the lowest impact, the 'minimum' is 22 kg $CO_2$/m$^2$ and the highest impact, the 'maximum', is 280 kg $CO_2$/m$^2$. By deducting the 'minimum' from the 'maximum', we find the 'range' for this element and issue — in this case for internal walls and climate change, it is 258 kg $CO_2$/m.

A, B and C ratings are then simply calculated for each specification and issue by assessing where the result lies within the range. An 'A' rating is obtained when the result is within the third of the range with the lowest environmental impact, a 'B' rating when it is within the middle third, and a 'C' rating when it is within the third of the range with the highest environmental impact.

For our internal wall and climate change example, the table below shows how the A, B and C ratings are defined.

| Green Guide ranges for internal walls — climate change (in kg $CO_2$) | | | | | |
|---|---|---|---|---|---|
| Minimum impact/m$^2$ | Maximum impact/m$^2$ | Range | 'A' rating range | 'B' rating range | 'C' rating range |
| 22 | 280 | 258 | 22–108 | 108–194 | 194–280 |

Taking our example specification, a painted, plasterboarded dense concrete blockwork wall, 100 mm thick, its total climate change impact over the 60-year life of the building was 29 kg $CO_2$/m$^2$. This is within the 'A' rating range of 22–108 kg $CO_2$ and this specification therefore gets an 'A' rating for climate change.

## *Generation of the Summary Rating for each specification*

In order to generate the Summary Rating for each specification, the individual impact results need to be weighted.

In the example above, each of the impacts is measured in different units — for example climate change in kilograms of $CO_2$ and waste in kilograms or tonnes of waste. These results cannot be weighted as they are all in different units — in order to weight them, we compare them to a common 'norm'; in the BRE Environmental Profiles Methodology this norm is the impact of a typical UK citizen.

The impacts of the norm are calculated by dividing the total impacts of the UK by the population. For climate change, this gives us an impact of 12,300 kg $CO_2$ per person, and for waste disposal 7.2 tonnes of waste.

By comparing each of our results for the specification to the norm, we obtain a 'normalised' result for each. These normalised values, which are dimensionless, can then be weighted using BRE weightings. The weighted values are now called Ecopoints, and can be compared directly across impact categories. More information on Ecopoints and weightings is provided on page 6. The table below shows the normalised values, weightings and Ecopoints values for our example specification.

| Climate change Ecopoints score for a painted, plasterboarded dense concrete blockwork wall, 100 mm thick, over a 60-year life. | | | | | |
|---|---|---|---|---|---|
| Issue | Impact (kg $CO_2$) | Norm (kg $CO_2$) | Normalised value | Weighting (%) | Ecopoint |
| Climate change | 29 | 12,300 | 0.00236 | 38 | 0.089 |

By undertaking this process for all the environmental issues for a specification, and adding the Ecopoints scores, the total Ecopoints score for each specification can be calculated. This is then done for all the specifications for the element, and A, B and C Summary Ratings are then generated by using the minimum and maximum overall Ecopoints score to generate the range, in exactly the same way as the ratings are generated for individual environmental issues.

# Appendix 3: Production of a BRE Environmental Profile for a material using the BRE Environmental Profiles Methodology

## Inventory analysis

First, a list of all the inputs and outputs or emissions from a process is compiled. This is known as an inventory. These data are then processed to make sure the rules of the LCA method chosen are applied. Using the BRE Methodology, inventory analysis takes account of any recycled input, any recycling or reuse of products after use, and allocation of environmental burdens to any co-products from product systems, such as the co-production of sodium hydroxide when manufacturing chlorine or the slags from metal refining.

## Impact assessment

Once the inventory has been produced for a product system, the burdens can be classified — that is they are assigned to the relevant environmental issues to which they contribute. For example, the emission of methane contributes to both global warming and summer smog. When all the burdens have been classified, they are then characterised. For each environmental issue, the characterisation process evaluates the strength of the classified burdens using a common unit.

For example, to characterise the effect of gases that have a global warming impact, we use the United Nations Inter-governmental Panel on Climate Change's 100-year Global Warming Potentials. The units we use to measure global warming are kilograms of $CO_2$ equivalent (kg $CO_2$ eq$^{100\ years}$). Under this system, compared to carbon dioxide ($CO_2$), methane has an effect 21 times greater for the same mass of emission. Therefore, emissions of 1 tonne $CO_2$ and 1 tonne methane, which have been classified as causing climate change, would be characterised to 1,000 and 21,000 kg $CO_2$ eq$^{100\ years}$ respectively.

Because each environmental issue has its own characterised unit, it is still hard to compare the different issues. The characterised impacts for each issue are therefore compared to the corresponding impacts of a 'norm' — the BRE Environmental Profiles Methodology uses the impacts of one UK citizen. This process is known as normalisation.

For example, the total climate change impact for the UK is approximately 721 million tonnes $CO_2$ eq$^{100\ years}$. Divided by the UK population (approximately 58.8 million), this gives climate change impact for one UK citizen of around 12,300 kg $CO_2$ eq$^{100\ years}$. The normalised impact of the emission of 1 tonne methane described above would therefore be 21,000/12,300 = 1.7.

Each impact now becomes a dimensionless proportion of the corresponding impact for one UK citizen and constructions can now be analysed by comparing their normalised impacts in the selected environmental issue categories.

The BRE Environmental Profile presents characterised and normalised data for each environmental issue. The normalised data can then be weighted using the BRE weighting factors to provide an Ecopoints score.

## Appendix 4: BREEAM case study

This case study follows the BREEAM assessment of an imaginary office building, to demonstrate the process of using *The Green Guide to Specification* within BREEAM 98 for Offices.

The materials section of BREEAM 98 for Offices makes up 10% of the total credits available for a design-stage assessment. This type of assessment can be used for both new developments and refurbishments.

Within BREEAM, there are 12 available credits relating to materials specification, one, relating to HCFCs, from the pollution section and 11 from the materials section. They are listed below — the final four relate to the use of *The Green Guide to Specification*.

| | |
|---|---|
| Specification of insultants avoids the use of ozone-depleting substances in manufacture and composition | 1 credit |
| No use of asbestos | 1 credit |
| Design of building incorporates dedicated storage space or space for skips for waste | 1 credit |
| Timber for key elements from sustainably managed sources | 1 credit |
| Timber panel products from sustainable managed sources | 1 credit |
| Reuse of > 50% of existing facades | 1 credit |
| Reuse of > 80% of major structure by building volume | 1 credit |
| Use of recycled aggregate or masonry in structure, slabs, road, etc. | 1 credit |
| At least 80% by area of upper floors slabs achieve an 'A' Summary Rating in *The Green Guide to Specification* | 1 credit |
| At least 80% by area of external wall specifications achieve an 'A' Summary Rating in *The Green Guide to Specification* | 1 credit |
| At least 80% by area of roof specifications achieve an 'A' Summary Rating in *The Green Guide to Specification* | 1 credit |
| At least 80% by area of windows specifications achieve an 'A' Summary Rating in *The Green Guide to Specification* | 1 credit |

Our imaginary building is square, the four different construction specifications (used for illustrative purposes) and their *Green Guide* Summary Ratings are as follows:

| | | |
|---|---|---|
| South façade | Aluminium composite cladding with an HCFC blown polyurethane foam insulation and a 100-mm dense blockwork inner skin | A |
| East façade | Polymeric render with glass wool reinforcement on dense blockwork, plasterboard with glass wool insulation | B |
| North façade | Timber-framed glazed curtain walling | A |
| West façade | Softwood cladding on dense blockwork with glass wool insulation | A |
| Windows | Hardwood windows | A |
| Roof | Aluminium double skin profiled roof, with pentane blown PU insulation on steel roof structure | A |
| Upper floors | Hollow precast reinforced slab with structural topping | B |
| Doors | Flush, chipboard face, softwood core. Chipboard for doors uses timber which is either from sustainably managed sources or 100% post-consumer waste. Softwood from sustainably managed sources | A |
| Ground floors | In-situ concrete over recycled aggregate fill | |

Aluminium insulated composite cladding with a 100-mm dense blockwork inner skin achieves an A rating. However, because it uses an HCFC blown insulation, the ozone depletion and climate change caused by the HCFCs would increase the impact of the specification such that its Summary Rating would be altered to a 'B' rating. Within BREEAM 98 for Offices, however, the loss of the 'Specification of insulants avoids the use of ozone-depleting substances in manufacture and composition' credit covers this increase in rating and the actual rating given in the table is therefore used for the assessment of the *Green Guide* credits.

Again, for the softwood rainscreen cladding, the actual rating of A is kept for the assessment of the *Green Guide* credit, even though the softwood is not from a sustainably managed source. This is because the loss of the 'Timber for key elements from sustainably managed sources' credit accounts for this.

The timber-framed glazed curtain walling is treated as a window element rather than an external wall element because it will not meet the functional unit relating to thermal resistance for external walls. The area of glazed curtain walling is discounted from the area of external walls used in the *Green Guide* external wall credit and is included in the area for the *Green Guide* windows credit.

Looking at each of the relevant *Green Guide* credits for our building in turn, we see the following:

| Specification of ZODP insulants | HCFC blown PU foam specified for south façade | No credit |
|---|---|---|
| No use of asbestos | New building with no asbestos | 1 credit |
| Design of building incorporates dedicated storage space or space for skips for waste | Area for recycling skips and paper recycling incorporated into design | 1 credit |
| Timber for key elements from sustainably managed sources | No evidence of sustainable sourcing provided for timber cladding for west façade | No credit |
| Timber panel products from sustainably managed sources | Chipboard for doors uses mix of post-consumer timber waste and timber from sustainably managed sources | 1 credit |
| Reuse of > 50% of existing façades | New development | No credit |
| Reuse of > 80% of major structure by building volume | New development | No credit |
| Use of recycled aggregate or masonry in structure, slabs, hard landscaping, etc. | Ground floor uses recycled aggregates as fill | 1 credit |
| *Green Guide* upper floor credit | 100% of the upper floors achieve a B rating | No credit |
| *Guide Guide* external wall credit | Only the south, east and west facades are assessed for this credit, the north façade being assessed as part of the windows credit; 66.6% of the external walls achieve an A rating and 33.3% achieve a B rating | No credit as 80% must achieve an A rating |
| *Green Guide* roof credit | 100% of the roof achieves an A rating | 1 credit |
| *Green Guide* window credit | 100% of the windows and glazed curtain walling achieve an A rating | 1 credit |

This building would achieve 6 of the available 12 credits relating to materials. The materials section accounts for 10% of the BREEAM rating, so this building would take forward 5% from the materials section towards the BREEAM rating.

## Appendix 5: Differences in environmental issues from previous editions

The table below shows the differences in issues covered in the second and third editions.

| Second edition | Third edition | Comment |
|---|---|---|
| Toxicity associated with manufacture | Human toxicity ecotoxicity | Assessed qualitatively in second edition. Now assessed quantitatively for whole life cycle |
| Toxicity associated with combustion | – | Assessed qualitatively in second edition. No longer assessed |
| Primary energy associated with extraction, production and transport | Climate change, acidification and fossil fuel depletion | Environmental impacts associated with energy use during extraction, production and transport now used rather than energy use as a proxy for environmental impact |
| Carbon dioxide | Climate change | Climate change includes the global warming potential of other gases such as methane or HCFCs in addition to carbon dioxide |
| VOCs (volatile organic compounds) | Summer smog | 'Summer smog' covers the relative contribution different types of VOCs make towards low-level photochemical ozone creation, which causes summer smog |
| $NO_x$ (nitrogen oxides) | Acidification and eutrophication | The impacts of $NO_x$ emissions are now measured |
| $SO_2$ (sulphur dioxide) | Acidification | The acidification potential of all emissions (e.g. $SO_x$, $NO_x$, HF, etc.) is now considered |
| Mineral resources | Mineral extraction | No change |
| Water resources | Water extraction | No change |
| Oil feedstock | Fossil fuel depletion | Now covers all fossil fuel depletion, not just use of oil as feedstock (e.g. for plastic) |
| Reserves of raw materials | | Previously a qualitative assessment. Not considered in this edition |
| Wastes generated | Waste disposal | No change |

The availability of data from the BRE Environmental Profiles project has meant that this edition has been able to move away from some of the more qualitative assessments given in previous editions. The new ratings now cover the twelve environmental issues included in the BRE Environmental Profiles, the overall Summary Rating and four ratings relating to recycling.

# Contacts and further information

For further information on BRE Environmental Profiles visit www.bre.co.uk/envprofiles.

For further information on BREEAM visit http://products.bre.co.uk/breeam/default.html.

For further information on the Envest software tool which provides more detailed analysis of building designs, including operational impacts of a building, visit www.bre.co.uk/envest.

For further information on green specification for housing and more domestic-scale construction see *The Green Guide to Housing Specification* by Anderson and Howard, published by BRE, 2000, available from www.brebookshop.com.

For further information on sourcing of reclaimed and recycled materials visit the Materials Information Exchange at www.bre.co.uk/waste.

# References

The range of sources drawn on was extensive and it was not considered practical to list all those used. A selection of key references appears below.

EC Regulation No. 2037/2000 of 29 June 2000. Official Journal, 29 Sept (L 244/1).

Anderson, J. and Edwards, S. (2000) Addendum to BRE Methodology for Environmental Profiles of Construction Materials, Components and Buildings. BRE, www.bre.co.uk/envprofiles/pdf/addendum.pdf.

Anderson, J. and Howard, N. (2000) The Green Guide to Housing Specification. BRE, Watford.

Anink, D., Boonstra, C. and Mak, J. (1996) Handbook of Sustainable Building. James & James, London.

CIRIA (1994) Environmental Issues in Construction (Energy and Resources Use), Vol. 2, Sect. 2. Construction Industry Research and Information Association, London.

CIRIA (1995) Environmental Impact of Building and Construction Materials. Vol. B Mineral Products; Vol. C Metals; Vol. D Plastics and Elastomers; Vol. E Timber and Timber Products; Vol. F Paints and Coatings, Adhesives and Sealants. Construction Industry Research and Information Association, London.

Coventry, S., Woolveridge, C. and Hillier, S. (1999) The Reclaimed and Recycled Construction Materials Handbook. Publication no. 513. Construction Industry Research and Information Association, London.

Department of Energy and Department of Industry (1979) Energy Audit Series. No. 5 Glass Industry. Department of Energy and Department of Industry.

DETR (1997) Continuing Survey of Road Goods Transport. DETR, London.

DETR (2000) Building a Better Quality of Life: A Strategy for More Sustainable Construction. DETR, London.

Dickie, I. and Howard, N. (2000) Assessing Environmental Impacts of Construction: Industry Consensus, BREEAM and UK Ecopoints. BRE Digest 446. BRE, Watford.

Ecobilan (1993) European Ecolable for Paints and Varnishes. Ecobilan, Paris.

Friends of the Earth (1996) The Good Wood Guide. Friends of the Earth, London.

HMSO (1998) The Digest of UK Energy Statistics 1998. Central Statistical Office, Stationery Office, London.

Howard, N., Edwards, S. and Anderson, J. (1999) BRE Methodology for Environmental Profiles of Construction Materials, Components and Buildings. BRE, Watford.

Institution of Mining and Metallurgy (1992) Minerals, Metals and the Environment. Elsevier, Oxford.

LCA databases: Simapro, www.pre.nl; IVAM, www.ivambv.uva.nl.

Lavers, A. and Shiers, D.E. (2000) Construction Law and Environmental Harm, Construction Management and Economics, Vol. 18, No. 8, pp. 893-902.

Metallgesellschaft AG (1992) Metal Statistics 1981-1991, 69th edn. Metallgesellschaft AG, Frankfurt-am-Main.

Potting, J. and Blok, K. (1993) The Environmental Life Cycle Analysis of Some Floor Coverings. In: Proc 1st Setac World Congress, Lisbon, March 1993. Department of Science, Technology and Society, Utrecht University, Padualaan.

Rao, S., Yates, A., Brownhill, D. and Howard, N. (2000) EcoHomes: the Environmental Rating for Homes. BRE, Watford.

UK Department of Energy (1984) Energy Use and Energy Efficiency in UK Manufacturing Industry up to the Year 2000, Vol. 2. UK Department of Energy, London.

Woolley, T, Kimmins, S., Harrison, P. and Harrison, R. (1997) Green Building Handbook. E&F Spon, London.

Woolley, T., Kimmins, S., (2000) Green Building Handbook Volume 2. E&F Spon, London.

# Index